Praises for *Draw Near*

Sherry Blankenship has, with *Draw Near*, come very close to bringing the reader face to face with the blessed Trinity. She has shown us that God is still good all the time, even in the bombardment of prayers through the darkest hours. This is a welcome and necessary message, well written and heartfelt. Sherry says at book's end, "I have decided to trust Jesus." She offers a pathway for others to follow. This is a compelling book. All who need answers should read it.

Palmer A. Reynolds, CEO
Phoenix Textile Corporation

Can God really be sovereign in the face of affliction? The answer, surprisingly, is a resounding "Yes!" Rarely is suffering examined so authentically and hopefully. Out of great loss came much joy – people whose lives were changed forever because of God's faithfulness to a red-haired wonder girl named Anna.

Jan Mueller, M.D.

Joy, sorrow, and faith mingle in this powerful story. Here is faith in action!

Lieutenant Commander David E. Mullis
SBC Military Chaplaincy

D0167857

Draw Near is a remarkable story, a lesson universal for all who struggle with life's challenges. I highly recommend this book and its valuable insights for those experiencing grief and for caregivers providing support.

Michael J. Cox, M.D.

Sherry Blankenship shares in an unforgettable and helpful way how God can bring good from the bad things in life. *Draw Near* provides an excellent resource for pastors and others who minister to people in need.

Hayes Wicker, D.Min.

ONE PILGRIM'S JOURNEY
THROUGH GRIEF
TO THE LAP OF JESUS

Draw Near

SHERRY BLANKENSHIP

TATE PUBLISHING *& Enterprises*

TATE PUBLISHING
& Enterprises

Tate Publishing is committed to excellence in the publishing industry. Our staff of highly trained professionals, including editors, graphic designers, and marketing personnel, work together to produce the very finest books available. The company reflects the philosophy established by the founders, based on Psalms 68:11,

"THE LORD GAVE THE WORD AND GREAT WAS THE COMPANY OF THOSE WHO PUBLISHED IT."

If you would like further information, please contact us:

1.888.361.9473 | www.tatepublishing.com

TATE PUBLISHING *& Enterprises*, LLC | 127 E. Trade Center Terrace Mustang, Oklahoma 73064 USA

Draw Near: One Pilgrim's Journey through Grief to the Lap of Jesus

Scripture quotations are taken from the *New American Standard Bible* ®, Copyright © 1960, 1962, 1963, 1968, 1971, 1972, 1973, 1975, 1977, 1995 by The Lockman Foundation. Used by permission. All rights reserved.

The opinions expressed by the author are not necessarily those of Tate Publishing, LLC.

Published in the United States of America

ISBN: 978-1-6024706-9-9

12.04.20

Anna and I were given three champion men—my prince, Dwight, and her brothers, Joshua and Jonathan. "The project" is lovingly and gratefully dedicated to them.

ACKNOWLEDGMENTS

Many thanks are due to those who inspired, encouraged, and helped with "the project."

Dwight, my husband and soulmate, shared his great heart every step of the way. His gift to Anna was her mother for fifteen months, and he is God's gift to me. Joshua and Jonathan, now men of valor like their Dad, continually warm my heart, affirming again our cherished bond as family. As Charlotte shared with Wilbur the pig about her spider eggs, you are my *magnum opus*, my greatest work.

For years Sharon Foster, Janet Wicker, Shugie Collingsworth, and Cindy Bush asked, then reminded, and then repeated their requests for this book. With strong, inspired determination, Janet and Sharon prayerfully forged ahead with me through the long process. Drs. Janet (Mueller) and Rob Hanson, Dave and Sandra Mullis, Matt and Nancy Newberry, and Carol Miller carefully read, noted, and advised.

How does one survive today's technical jungle without brilliant friends? Help from "Miss Dale" Morrow and Steve Price made computer modifications possible.

Many have heard me say in hallways and at bedsides, "Nurses are the heroines of the world." I thank God for each of you genuine servants.

When Ron and Dottie Weinel lived in St. Louis, Dottie prayed and Bro. Ron dug deep to help many people. Dottie's teaching of Blackaby's "crisis of belief" has bolstered my faith through life's storms.

God has used countless patients to train my mind and spirit in service as a chaplain and friend. Jesus is my example. You are my tutors. Young Andrew Benecke became more than a patient. Andrew, the remarkable only son of Dr. Jim and Barbara, came to saving faith in Christ and was baptized with his dad by Dwight at Parkway while in the throes of wrenching osteosarcoma. Jim recently jotted an insightful note to Dwight:

"One of the challenges we face as followers of Christ is to show the world how to be sad. I buried my only child; I would be brain dead if I were not sad. I sorrow in the reality of the hope that I have in Christ, but it is not mitigated sorrowing. If someone is worth loving, they are worth grieving over. The Christian experience is not the experience of being removed from the rigors of life; it is the experience of knowing that even though this pain will last for all of my life, I must set this experience in the light of the vastness of God's eternity. In the words of a Puritan, 'I am besieged, not captured.'"

Barb and Jim, thank you for sharing Andrew with us and for allowing the grace of Christ to permeate your mourning. One day He will wipe all our tears away.

If ever a church epitomized the biblical metaphor of a "household of faith," our Parkway family does. Pastor and I love you with our whole hearts. May the grace of God abound more and more as He works in and through you.

Table of Contents

Preface 11

"Memories" 13

Foundations 15

Changes 25

Smiles 31

Challenges 37

Hope 53

Questions 65

Tribulation 79

Blessings 93

Hooray! 113

Shadows 123

Passage 151

Rituals 157

Grappling 165

"Goodbye" 175

"Why Do People Die?" 177

Epilogue 179

Reflections 185

This is the story of one mother's journey, condensed from four handwritten journals along with memories and impressions. Some of the pages bear tear stains. Between others are tucked little scraps from the day – a rainbow photo, Mr. Miller's special gum wrapper, a jotted note or poem.

The purpose of this writing is to share hope and encouragement with other pilgrims. Our family survived grief and loss. With God's help, you can, too.

When your only prayer is, "Lord, help me," He hears and is there.

The year after Anna died, our friend Mary Engelbreit surprised us with an original drawing, which we received on Thanksgiving Day. Mary drew Anna sitting outside sketching flowers, her name "Anna Joy" visible on the sketchpad. A golden shaft of light shines down on her, and the caption reads, "Draw near to God, and He will draw near to you." James 4:8.

The promise is true. He is always present, always waiting for us to "draw near."

It is a reminder we have returned to many times, including the days and weeks spent writing this book.

In our "empty nest" years, with Dwight's and our sons' encouragement I entered post-graduate studies, became a board certified chaplain, and am now blessed to serve a wonderful hospital in our community, Missouri Baptist Medical Center. Our story, lived and recorded before clinical training, is from a mother's perspective. It is followed by "Reflections" on grief, both from our own pilgrimage, further study, and experiences of others with whom I have since walked. I pray it will help you sense the nearness of the faithful Father who loved us first and best.

"Weeping may last for the night, but. . . joy comes in the morning." Psalm 30:5.

"Memories"

By Anna Joy Blankenship

When yesterday seems so far away,

And tomorrow will never come,

Memories slip into my heart.

Bright and warm,

They remind me of the simple beauty
of times past.

Dreams and ambition desert in your hour
of loneliness,

But memories never leave you.

They creep into a secret chamber in
the corner of your soul.

A bitter-sweet pain escorts memories,
Causing ache or comfort.

Tears–smiles

Hurt–happiness

Memories.

FOUNDATIONS

It was a hot Texas afternoon, the bright sun just beginning to lower as Dallas rush hour traffic, bumper to bumper, crept and swerved and halted along a maze of intertwining freeways. One dot in that picture was a little green hatchback Vega with white interior nicknamed "the Pickle," every inch packed with all the earthly possessions of its driver, a twenty-two-year-old Southern belle who had never been to Texas and never seen a freeway. She had already driven six hundred miles or so that day and was not adept at reading maps. Southwestern Seminary was in Fort Worth, which was supposed to be next door to Dallas. It had to be around here somewhere.

After several wrong turns and more than a few screeches and honking horns, the weary driver pulled off at the next exit, stopped on the shoulder with cars and trucks whizzing by, and cried. Boo-hooed. And sniffled a prayer, "Father, help. PLEASE show me the way." After a couple of minutes, she deemed it "enough," blew her nose, and eased back onto the highway heading west toward the setting sun.

The year was 1974. Not many hours later I was awed to gaze through the Pickle's front windshield down a long grassy promenade toward the imposing domed administration building of Southwestern Seminary.

I sighed at the realization of arrival. Of promise. Of God's faithfulness.

Thank You, Father. Thank You.

The Southwestern years were a strategic part of the Lord's plan. While earning a master's degree, I also learned to know and trust God through the teaching examples of faithful professors, fellowship with other students, and experiencing a life of dependence upon Him. It was here that my handsome prince, Dwight Blankenship, entered the picture. We courted in New Mexico where he served on summer staff at Glorieta Conference Center while I was the first summer children's intern at Hoffmantown church in Albuquerque. Back at Southwestern we completed studies, became engaged, and sought the Lord's direction for our next step.

I worked for the Foreign Mission Board while Dwight took a temporary position at an industrial pipe production foundry. We prayed for clear direction and were soon blessed with Dwight's call to his first pastorate.

During our engagement I saw a Fort Worth gynecologist and was told by him that it was doubtful we would be able to have children. Stunned by this disappointing prospect, I left the doctor's office and drove to the pipe factory to find Dwight. He joined me outside the plant, heard my anxious sorrow, and kindly reminded me that the Bible says God "opens and closes the womb." If He willed us to have children, we would, one way or another.

June 24, 1978, our seminary pastor, Dr. D. L. Lowrie, pronounced us man and wife in my hometown, Hattiesburg, Mississippi, and we moved into the parsonage provided by the loving congregation of First Baptist Church, Alba, Texas. What an ideal community for the newlywed pastor and his bride. They taught him how to pastor and showed me how to support his ministry, foundations we have always treasured.

With Alba's official population at 505, mail was not delivered to the house; we walked to the tiny brick post office on the square and asked postmaster Elwood for our mail. He knew everyone in town and everyone's business. "Another letter from Fort Worth. Who do you know over there?"

Haisten's Grocery sold peanut butter in glass mugs with handles that yielded quite a collection of drinking glasses as well as many peanut butter sandwiches. Watermelons and sweet potatoes were the cash crops and we enjoyed lots of both from generous farmers in the congregation.

Two and a half years later Dwight was called to Southside Baptist Church in Palestine, Texas. We had been praying that God would give us a baby. Hannah's prayer in the Old Testament, I Samuel Chapter One, became one of my favorite Bible stories.

We did not know then that God was already preparing the nest in Palestine. Soon after the move we conceived and not long after that learned that we were expecting not one baby but three.

Triplets.

It was true! There were three.

Early in the pregnancy it became apparent that I might not be able to carry the babies. They were due around the first of December, and Dr. Peyton Luckett hoped for a November delivery. He initially ordered bed rest at home and then surprised us at an office visit in August with orders to go directly to the hospital for admission with the bed tilted head down, feet up.

Tyler was fifty miles from our home in Palestine. Dwight came as often as he could while pastoring the congregation there. We prayed that God would use the time for good purpose and that the babies would be strong and healthy. For two months I remained "upside down" with time to rest in the Lord and cherish those three little ones growing inside.

Since the first sensory perception in utero is audial, a baby hears his/her mother and comes into the world knowing her voice. Every morning I read the Bible aloud and prayed by name for Joshua, Jonathan, and Anna Joy. One morning the nurse came in as we were reading and praying.

"Do you do this every morning?" she asked. After that she and others often joined us.

On September 23 the nurse observed a slight flinch.

"Are you in labor?"

"Oh, no, not real labor; nothing to worry about."

She seemed O.K. with that, but soon afterward Dr. Luckett came in, quickly responding to her call from the nurses' station.

His friendly manner almost masked his urgency. "Any contractions?" he asked while pressing his hand to my extended tummy.

"Not really."

"Well, I can feel it. You're in labor."

It was not like the movies. No thrashing and screaming. This was labor?

Dr. Luckett ordered an IV to stop the labor and explained that I would need to move down the hall to a labor room equipped with special monitoring equipment. Could I please call Dwight first to let him know I would not be there in case he called?

It was late Wednesday afternoon, church supper night. I quickly called the church phone number, and a fellow in line for supper answered on the hall phone. No, he didn't see Pastor. Yes, he would tell him that I would be spending the night in a labor room. "Now, remember, be sure to tell him I'm NOT in real labor; no reason to come racing to Tyler; just wanted him to know. Got it? O.K."

The labor room, brightly lit, all white with stainless steel equipment, was stark and a little unnerving. In a short while the door opened and in rushed my flushed, worried prince. The message he had received: "Sherry's in labor!"

Through the long night he stayed, and our kind Dr. Luckett checked in often, too.

By morning he regretfully told us that labor had slowed but not completely stopped.

He felt the best course was to send me to Dallas immediately so that, just in case the babies should come, there would be a larger NICU, newborn intensive care unit, adequate to care for three very premature babies.

After quick good-byes I was loaded into an ambulance with one accompanying nurse and a nervous driver who made record time! With my enormous belly, the only way to lie on a narrow cot in a speeding ambulance was sideways. As we careened toward Baylor Hospital in Dallas, the nurse somehow kept me from rolling to the floor while also managing clanging glass IV bottles overhead.

Poor Dwight hastily emptied the Tyler hospital room of two months of cards, books, plants, gifts, and other paraphernalia, stuffed all into our unairconditioned red Volkswagen Beetle "Chigger" (red bug), and trailed the speeding ambulance to Dallas. When he arrived, the Baylor medical staff, prepping me for delivery, asked if he would like to join me. Unprepared for that possibility, Dwight, without benefit of classes or coaching, bravely gulped, "Yes."

Scrubbed, gowned, and gloved, Dwight witnessed the C-section births of our babies–Joshua Dwight, Anna Joy, and Jonathan Clark. It was September 24, 1981.

The boys each weighed 3 lb. 6 oz. and Anna 2 lb. 14 oz. They were tiny, fragile bundles of life struggling to breathe with premature lungs, and they were precious to us.

We thanked God and prayed for His hand of mercy on our babies whose medical conditions were critical. Jonathan, Joshua, and Anna Joy were whisked away to the NICU where hours turned to days and days to weeks of roller coaster ups and downs.

In pleading with the Lord for their lives, I made two promises. First, if He let them live, I would always remember to say "Thank You" like the one leper in the New Testament who turned back to thank Jesus. Second, if He would let the babies live, I would not complain about taking care of them. By God's mercy, they did survive, and they were such wonderful children it was easy to keep both promises.

Typical of preemies, the babies initially lost weight before beginning to grow again. Anna's light hair seemed to have a reddish cast; and even as the smallest, she was spunky. The nurses would carefully position her in the isolette with tubes and wires arranged just so. Invariably, at next glance, Anna had scooted crossways with her spindly, toothpick legs protruding from the white snowball of diaper, her dainty feet propped on the unit's round porthole. This happened so many times the nurses laughed and said, "That's Anna!"

One day this two-pound wonder baby pulled out her own feeding tube and never needed it again.

Eventually the three babies stabilized and graduated to an intermediate nursery and finally were scheduled for transfer back to Mother Francis Hospital in Tyler to "fatten up."

The week before Thanksgiving, Joshua and Jonathan reached five pounds and were allowed to come home. The next week Anna came, too. At last we were at home as a family. It was truly a season of thanks.

Even with Apnea monitors and lots of bottles and diapers, those were happy, blessed days. To avoid respiratory infection, at the neonatal pediatrician's recommendation the babies were quarantined at home until the Sunday after Easter.

This meant that Mommy was at home with babies every day, so it was easy to stay on a schedule and care for our little family. Our only ventures out were to see Dr. Joe Bates in Tyler or to the photography studio, also considered a necessity! Kind neighbors and church members helped in every conceivable way, and we were most grateful.

One Sunday evening when my parents were visiting, I went to church with Dwight while they stayed with the babies. They reported later that one of the boys began crying and so my mother searched the refrigerator for his bottle but couldn't remember the system (pink for Anna, blue for Joshua, yellow for Jonathan). As she was explaining the predicament to my dad, baby Anna crawled to the open refrigerator, pulled up, and reached toward the correct bottle for her crying brother. Anna's attention and care for her brothers became a life pattern.

When Anna was seven years old, she came to me one evening with earnest concern that she wanted to ask Jesus into her heart. Because she was so young, I wondered if she could understand the concept of her need and Christ's provision, but she sincerely expressed it and then prayed giving her heart to Him. Dwight and I asked her to wait for believer's baptism until we felt she was old enough to be sure of her commitment and to better understand what it meant. She agreed and sweetly obeyed.

A year later during second grade I received a call one evening from the children's teacher, Mrs. Ellis. She shared that during recess that day Anna had come in from the playground with her friend Amber. Amber wanted to ask Jesus into her heart, and Anna had told her they should find Mrs. Ellis who would help Amber.

Mrs. Ellis described looking down into the flushed, happy faces of those two little girls and wondering what to do. She had grown up in a Christian home but over the years had gradually grown away from the foundations of her faith. Now, she was literally "face to face" with the faith she remembered from childhood. The following Sunday Mrs. Ellis and her family were in church and chose to follow Christ, too. After their professions, we told Anna it was probably time for her to be baptized.

One of Anna's strongest life influences was her great-grandmother whom she named "Sweet Granny." They called themselves "snuggle buddies," sleeping together at every opportunity. Sweet Granny, whose hair in our memory was always in a thick, white bun, said as a child her hair had been red, much like Anna's. The bond between those two dear souls was strong and true.

Once when Granny came to visit us in Texas, she told how she was saved when the circuit riding preacher came to her community. She was baptized in the Okatoma River and told us that when she came up out of the water she saw all her sins flowing down the river.

I interjected, "Granny, you didn't have any sin," to which she replied, "Child, everybody has sins, but Jesus washed them all away."

Dwight completed doctoral studies at Southwestern Seminary, graduating–again–May, 1986. Anna explained that Daddy was now "Dr. Blankenship," but he did not give shots.

The Palestine years were filled with treasured memories and relationships. Life was very, very good. With Dwight's call to Paris, Texas came many tears, but he faithfully obeyed and the rest of us trooped along.

CHANGES

School, sports, music, church activities, and many dear friends helped the children quickly adjust as we were welcomed into the Paris community. They seemed to try everything, with Anna as the ringleader. She played softball, volleyball, basketball, and ran track. A bright, disciplined student, Anna always had time and patience to help her brothers and friends with their schoolwork, too. She was elected to student council, sang in the choir, and organized a community-wide food collection for needy families.

Thrilled to win several essay contests, Anna dreamed of becoming an author like her favorite, L.M. Montgomery who wrote *Anne of Green Gables.* We framed a copy of the first check she received as reward for her writing.

One recurring theme in several of Anna's poems and essays was sickness and death. Dwight and I thought this a bit odd since she had always been healthy and we had not experienced death in our immediate family.

Dwight bought two beautiful acres in the county, and a gracious deacon contractor built a barn of a house large enough for our three children and all of their friends who romped in and out for baseball, basketball, trampoline, or inside games. Their favorite was "hide and seek" in the dark. It was also a great place for weddings, fellowship gatherings, and heart-to-heart prayer times.

After five years in Paris, Dwight was called to Parkway Baptist Church in St. Louis to assume the pastorate in January, 1995. As he announced his resignation to the Paris congregation, we put the house on the market and began the transition process, including a family trip to Texas A&M University with alumnae Susan and Jim Davis.

Anna experienced Aggieland football and culture with the goal of returning in a few years for college. The Aggies won her heart.

The following week was to be Thanksgiving and a big Saturday wedding at the church. In the wee hours of Thursday morning, Thanksgiving Day, we were awakened in the darkness by screaming shrieks of smoke alarms. There was no scent or sight of smoke, but the loud screeching persisted. It was Thanksgiving; I had probably left something in the oven.

A quick sprint downstairs to the kitchen, and sure enough, the smell of smoke was unmistakable. To my surprise, however, the oven was off and cold. Smoke billowed in around the door to the garage. Dwight opened and closed it in a flash. Both cars were on fire. The phone was ringing from the security alarm company to confirm that there was a fire. Fire trucks were on the way. Get everyone out.

Sweet Anna was at the top of the stairs to see what was wrong. "The house is on fire," I replied, hopping up toward her. "Get your brothers out, and I'll get the pictures!" (Can you imagine that? It gets worse.)

"Be sure everyone has shoes on. There are stickers in the yard." The house was on fire, we were all upstairs, and Mom was concerned about stickers in the yard! At any rate, Anna quickly got her brothers up and out, all with shoes, Josh with his glasses and Jonathan nabbing his baseball card album. Dad went out and started fighting the fire with the garden hose awaiting the fire trucks. Mom raced down the hall collecting precious baby photos and followed them out.

Several years earlier Anna had come home from school reporting that every family needed a fire plan "just in case." What was our fire plan? We agreed that in case of fire, we would all meet at the big tree in the front yard. We had not discussed it since, but that night as predetermined we all met at the big tree in the front yard. It has become a spiritual symbol in the years afterward that I recall often.

I made a few more runs into the house for picture albums and a wooden box of negatives in the music room just left of the entry. (Later, one of the men tried to lift the heavy box in the front yard and asked who in the world had been able to carry it out.) The last thing I could rescue was Sweet Granny's sewing machine from the dining room.

To be inside one's house as it burns is surreal. Our home, the family nest, the secure place of refuge and nurturing, was now strangely familiar yet alarmingly ominous. All my senses were skewed. A yellowish caste tinted surroundings, an acrid smell permeated, and strange sounds crackled as windows popped and crashed.

Faintly from outside I heard Anna screaming "Mom." As I pulled Granny's sewing machine out the door and over the porch threshold, I knew there would be no more going in. The children and I huddled together under the big tree as Dwight continued to fight the fire through exposed, bulging sides of the still-closed garage doors. Paint cans were exploding with loud booms that awakened neighbors who gathered on the lawn in pre-dawn darkness.

One lady moaned, "Oh, your beautiful home." My immediate heart response was, "The house is burning, but the home is intact."

All the stuff could go. The five of us were safe and together.

Brave firemen from the rural volunteer fire department arrived and took over the flaming scene. After the fire appeared to be out, it blazed again and they returned. The skill and dedication of those men earned our greatest respect and gratitude as did the care of many church members who helped salvage smoky remains from the house. Parishioners carried out sooty furniture and blackened household things, offered to launder clothing items that seemed usable, and comforted us with the love of Christ. Just like the commercial, our State Farm Insurance lady was right there in the early morning with adjoining hotel rooms already reserved. She then guided and helped us through every step of the recovery process.

Since it was Thanksgiving Day, most stores were closed, but the Davises found a way to purchase Fruit of the Loom cotton sweat suits, underwear, combs, and toothbrushes for each of us. Jonathan said he would never wear his sweats, so Mom got two. For the beautiful wedding Dwight wore a shirt and pants, borrowed Sunday shoes, and a blue choir robe.

Dwight told his friend and doctor Bert Strom he was concerned that I might have inhaled too much smoke running back into the house. Would he please listen to my lungs? I felt fine but went along. Later at the office, my lungs were clear, but I did take that opportunity to nonchalantly ask, "You know, as long as we're here, does Dwight's neck seem a little puffy to you?"

I had just been buying Dwight larger shirts, thinking the increase in his collar size was because we had both put on a little weight. Bert gently felt the area and knew immediately there was a problem. Soon afterward we were in the local community hospital where a tumor and part of Dwight's thyroid were removed.

Late afternoon following surgery, Dwight, pale and motionless, was wheeled back into his hospital room where I waited (wearing Fruit of the Loom sweats). Standing beside his bed, I could look across to the window and out at the sunset. Alone with my sleeping husband, in the quietness I pondered our situation.

There was no house. No car. Virtually no clothes. No church—we were in between. And Dwight might have cancer.

This was a rare moment, a watershed in my life unlike any other before or since. "Father," I realized. "There is nothing. There is not one thing of this world left to claim."

Our lot seemed like that of a new baby born into the world naked and utterly dependent. There was not one thing to claim except God, our Father and Good Shepherd.

And there He was.

He was enough.

I wish I could describe the overwhelming sense of peace in that moment. Words cannot tell it. There was no fear, only peace. The peace that passes understanding. I and my family were held securely, tenderly in everlasting arms that would never let us go. It felt as if we were swaddled in one of Granny's soft quilts. I will never forget it.

The epiphany of that evening was a life marker, a stone of remembrance set down as preparation for things to come.

Dwight's pathology report came back "pre-cancerous." He would be fine! We rejoiced and thanked God for the good news. The Lord provided a rental house, Paris folks gave us a mini-van dubbed the "Mama Bus," and Dwight could recuperate in days already scheduled for transition to St. Louis.

December offered family time to regroup. We celebrated Christmas with renewed commitments to the Savior whose birth in a stable brought us eternal promise.

January one Dwight began his new ministry in St. Louis. The rest of us would remain in Texas to rebuild the house for market and to work through the insurance process. Dwight drove away with a sure knowledge of God's call and provision for our family. We would make it.

The following months were busy as the children continued school and sports.

A true gift beyond measure, Mel and Sue Young, whose daughter Beth Ann was Anna's best friend, invited us to stay with them while Dwight was away. Anna roomed with Beth Ann, and Josh and Jonathan slept on an air mattress next to my twin bed in the spare room. Our belongings were minimal and our fellowship abundant. By God's grace we got to be together with Daddy almost every other week, either in St. Louis or Dallas or Paris. The Lord continued to supply every need.

SMILES

Lest the reader consider the Blankenships a stoic, somber lot, let me assure you we have always had more than our share of fun. This chronicle would not be complete without adding a few.

From the beginning our three children, though begotten at the same time from the same womb, were unique little individuals. Joshua was blonde like his father, Jonathan fair with dark hair like mine, and Anna had thick copper curls—a redhead. Life was never dull or boring. Anna, the leader; Jonathan, the thinker; and Joshua, the innovator. Each one brought special gifts to our family. Every day was a gift of learning and growing together.

When the children had chicken pox, they took turns, one at a time, a very l. . . o. . . n. . . g process of breakouts and recovery. By the time Jonathan, our third patient, broke out, all of us were getting a little stir crazy, so we decided to have a chicken pox party. As young friends were called, we asked their mothers if they had ever had chicken pox. If so, they were invited to the party.

As guests arrived, their faces were dotted with red lipstick "pox." They decorated paper plates and balloons as chicken pox faces and relished sugar cookies with red candies. Everyone had a good time. There's always a reason to celebrate.

Early one winter morning I was awakened by a small voice right next to my bedside. Opening my eyes, there stood Jonathan in his footed fleece pajamas with a bewildered look on his face.

"What's wrong, Jonathan? Did you have a bad dream?"

In the early morning light he held out his small hands, and I was as puzzled as he to behold the tops of his hands—vivid, glaring, emerald green! Sitting up to take a closer look, I quickly realized they had been carefully decorated sometime during the night with a green colored marker by his same-age roommate who now, in daylight, slept soundly. That was one of many episodes involving Joshua's minimal need for sleep.

As young male adventurers five or six years old, Joshua and Jonathan decided to protect our family from the danger of wild bears by engineering a bear trap in our two acre back yard. They chose a spot well away from the house and started digging, borrowing their Daddy's shovels from the garage.

It was good exercise and harmless fun for two energetic little boys. Who could have imagined the size hole they could accomplish? Actually, a crater about five feet wide and several feet deep, large enough to hold any bear wandering into the neighborhood. Pleased with phase one, they then gathered pine boughs and carefully laid them across the hole as a camouflage from the eyes of some unsuspecting bear.

Thrilled with the success of their enterprise, they burst into the kitchen and Mama went out with them to see. It really was impressive. I went back inside for the camera and took a picture of the proud duo standing beside their creation.

As the day went on, our attention turned to other activities. Suppertime conversation included reports on the bear trap. So far, all was well.

The boys checked the bear trap several times on following days, but rain storms often dictated indoor play. A week or two later, for some unknown reason, Dwight walked out to the back portion of the lot to check something, and before he knew it, he slipped into a cold, wet, muddy hole.

The bear trap worked! But not for the intended victim. Uh-oh. Not funny at that point but laughable in later years for sure. Needless to say, the next project was filling the bear trap.

Note: Some details of this family legend have been debated, but this is how it is usually retold.

One Thanksgiving we had plans to join another family for the holiday meal and my assignment was homemade pies. The day before, I spent most of the morning baking the usual assortment and set them on the kitchen counter to cool. Coming through later, I noticed that one of the pies had an obvious and deep finger swoop through the center. Uhhh!! The children were called in.

"Anna, did you do this?"

"No ma'am, Mama. I didn't do it."

"Jonathan, did you?"

"No ma'am, Mama. I didn't do that."

"Joshua?"

A long pause, and then, "Are you going to spank whoever did it?"

Many of our family memories involve my forgetfulness. Once, leaving the children with a fine church couple, we took a passel of young retired couples to a Dallas hotel for the Texas Evangelism Conference, two days of inspiring sermons and music. When we got into our hotel room, Dwight called back to the church to check in with secretary Joyce. Lots of amiable church folks were milling about in our room and the hallway, something like summer youth camp. Joyce asked, "Have you opened your suitcase yet?"

"No," he replied.

"I'll hold while you open your suitcase."

Relaying this message to me, Dwight held the telephone while I followed Joyce's instruction.

"What does she mean? Has someone played a trick on us?"

Upon opening the suitcase, truth was readily apparent. On top lay, neatly folded, a little pink flannel Cabbage Patch gown and two GI Joe zip-up footed pajamas. I had taken our suitcase to the baby sitter's and brought the children's suitcase with us.

Another traveling time, Anna accompanied me to a college campus where I was to be the Bible teacher for Fellowship of Christian Athletes national girls' camp. When the initial invitation call had come from their distant office, I had thanked them sincerely but apprehensively explained that I had no athletic ability at all. Did they understand that I was a fluffy cookie baker?

Yes, they knew that. Professional women athletes would lead training sessions, but they wanted a home-and-family type to lead morning Bible studies. Reluctantly I agreed, based on our family mantra, "Always say yes unless there's a good reason to say no."

Anna excitedly came along as my roommate in the leadership dormitory. She could hardly wait. When we arrived at the college and found registration, I timidly approached the desk surrounded by trim, tanned, smiling young women who looked at me quizzically, "May we help you?"

Upon introduction there was quick cordial recognition and a kind offer to bring in our luggage. We went out to the parked mini-van and opened the back to see the space empty. I had been so nervous and pre-occupied, our suitcases had been left at home!

After the fire, the children and I remained in Paris to oversee rebuilding the house. One day after checking on building progress, I stopped at Ken's Quik Stop on the county road nearby for gas and then headed back toward town. It was a beautiful East Texas day. Driving along the lush green fields and farms dotted with houses, it was with a grateful heart for many blessings during our twenty-one years in the Lone Star State. Passing drivers waved from their pick-up trucks and I smiled and waved back. We surely would miss this kind of down home friendliness in the move "north."

Nearing the loop around town, one man in a passing truck seemed to be motioning. I didn't understand, but decided to pull over to see if there might be a problem. Dwight was away and we did not need car problems with the new van.

Climbing out, I didn't notice anything at first, and then gasped at the strangest sight. Sticking out of the gas tank was the nozzle from the filling station, still held in the opening like a six-shooter. Stretching down the highway, its long black hose and attached train trailed behind the van like a gigantic umbilical cord.

Yes, odd as it seemed, there it was. No wonder people were waving and smiling. Hmmm. What to do now.

The white "Mama Bus" was new. If I lugged all that apparatus in the van, it would smell of gasoline. No, that wouldn't work. There was only one thing to do.

I climbed back in the driver's seat, made a u-turn in the highway, and started back in the opposite direction. Now, the weird sight was facing oncoming traffic.

Yes, yes, as they waved. I know. Good morning to you, too.

Back at Ken's, I pulled onto the black-top surface and stepped out. Awkwardly grasping the nozzle in my left hand, I tried to scoop up the rest over my right arm as graciously as possible. As I approached the counter, the eyes of the young attendant were fixed with wonder on the scene before him.

"Excuse me, but I believe this belongs to you."

"Yes ma'am."

"Can you fix it?"

"No ma'am."

"Mmm. Well, what would you like me to do with it?"

"Just put it down over there," he nodded toward the door.

I did as he suggested; then took a deep breath, looked straight ahead, and drove quickly away.

A month or two later, we attended a Christian worship gathering where at one point in the service congregants were encouraged to turn and greet one another. As I smiled and shook the hand of the man behind me, he smiled in return at the introduction.

"I know who you are," he said. "My name is Ken."

CHALLENGES

In May, 1995, our rebuilt house was nearing completion. Choir and band concerts, baseball tournaments, and other rituals signaled the end of the school year, and we were more than ready to be together as a family. Mrs. Crook, temporarily in the Texas Valley, allowed us to rent her house for the brief remaining time. She and so many others were kind, but it was time to move north, even if the house was not yet finished.

At the annual school awards night, Jonathan, Anna, and her friend Kristi Swasko took home multiple academic awards. Jonathan and Kristi tied for the Math Award.

On our way home that evening Joshua helpfully explained his brother's situation. "You know, it's really not fair for Jonathan. Kristi's Mama is smart!"

Dwight and Earl Brasfield, a Parkway parishioner, were driving down to Paris to transport Dwight's books from the church study. Josh would return to St. Louis with them, and as soon as Jonathan finished his current baseball tournament, he and Anna and I would move, too. In preparation, I made appointments for medical and dental check-ups and updated tetanus shots for the children.

Anna had been running a low-grade fever and felt unusu-ally tired, which troubled me. Aunt Dorisy said when Anna was at her house in Dallas, at one point she just laid her little head down on the kitchen table. Even so, she maintained all A's, ran track, and participated in many activities besides our frequent week-end trips to meet Dad, all without complaint.

Anna and Dr. Tom Cutrell laughed when I asked him to order a blood test checking for anemia. I replied that if every-thing was alright, he could order sugar pills for Mama.

My seminary roommate Cheri and her internist husband David Jordan arrived with their darling girls that weekend to say good-bye. I mentioned Anna's phantom fever, but there were no other glaring symptoms. She felt tired and achy, probably related to the tetanus shot. We had lived with Sue and Dr. Mel and he had never noticed a problem either. She was the picture of health. Still, I was uneasy.

For Dwight's Father's Day gift we scheduled a Sears pho-tography session for Sunday afternoon after church in dress-up clothes. Anna did not feel well enough to attend church with us that day and the portraits were cancelled.

Dwight and Earl Brasfield arrived late Sunday night. Mr. Brasfield spent the night at the rental house with us and convinced us that life in St. Louis would be great! Later, Dwight whispered to me that our new friend was a cancer patient who in privacy administered his own chemotherapy treatments.

Joshua was excited about going on to St. Louis with Dad and Mr. Brasfield.

After they left Tuesday morning, Anna and I drove to the pediatric clinic for a blood draw. Late Wednesday afternoon Dr. Tom called back ordering a second blood test for Anna. He said they were checking something and needed another look. Anna and I went for the draw, then picked up Jonathan and stopped for an early supper. When we returned to the rental house, Dr. Tom's car was in the driveway and he sat in the car (he told us later) crying. Inside the house, gravely, sadly, he shared the worst news we ever could have imagined. Anna had leukemia. Raging, advanced leukemia.

I was stunned. Surely this was not possible. Not Anna. We needed a second opinion. Tom had already sought multiple counsels and all had confirmed the dreadful diagnosis. He was so sorry. He had called his wife Debbi and friend Susan Davis who were on their way over. He called Dwight in St. Louis to break the terrible news and also contacted St. Louis Children's Hospital to set up admission. There was no time to lose. We would leave tonight.

I made a few calls asking for prayer. The doorbell was ringing. We hastily packed a few things. Laden with snacks for our trip, Kathy McMonigle and Helen Ledbetter came in and straightened the house with promises to send our other belongings by mail. Jim Davis gassed up the Mama Bus. I checked in on Anna's room where someone was helping her sort treasured possessions. When I peeked into Jonathan's room, he was kneeling beside his bed in prayer.

Anna, Jonathan, and I took a few minutes alone to cry and pray. She called some friends to say "good-bye." Then all of us gathered in the living room, held hands in a circle, and I somehow prayed aloud. It was 9:30 as we headed out, driving north in the darkness of night. My heart was heavy.

Debbi and Susan took turns driving as Jonathan and Anna and I huddled together in the back. None of us slept much; it was a long night.

Anna, thirteen, was, of course, afraid, but even in that frightening time she possessed a kind of grace unusual in one so young. We held each other tightly.

I could not honestly assure Anna everything would be all right, but I did promise her that we would stick together. Whatever the coming days might bring, she would never be alone. By God's grace that was a promise kept.

Driving through the night, we arrived in St. Louis about 7:30 AM, picked up Dwight at his mother's house, hugged Josh, and then proceeded to St. Louis Children's Hospital for Anna's first bone marrow test. This is a very painful procedure no matter how skilled the doctor, and Dr. Shenoy was. A drug called Versed was used for Anna, a potion which, at its best, serves as an amnesiac so the patient will not remember the awful ordeal.

As Anna lay on the table at Children's for the bone marrow test, her gentle face looked up at me, groggy under the influence of drugs and the all-night drive. "Mom," she asked in a slurred voice, "Why are you upside down?"

She must have seen the expression in my eyes, because she added, "Mom, God has not given us a spirit of fear, but of power and of love and of a sound mind."

Then she added, "You know, Mom, the horse is made ready for the day of battle, but the victory belongs to the Lord."

These verses came from the mouth of a child in the most extreme circumstances, a child unable to even think clearly. The Bible says, "Out of the abundance of the heart, the mouth speaks." Anna's words that day reminded me of the importance of inscribing God's Word on the hard-drive of our hearts.

Later, after the test, she did not remember any of it, but when I asked her about the "horse verse," she reminded me that she had read Proverbs 21:31 one night and had come into my bedroom to show me. She decided it would be her track verse, to be memorized and repeated while in position before each race. At every track meet since then, as she prepared in the final minutes before a race, she would look down the track, focus, and quote that verse. Now when under Versed, that which had been tucked into her dear little heart came flowing out.

The bone marrow test confirmed Dr. Tom's earlier diagnosis. Anna did have leukemia with eighty percent "blasts" (bad cells) in her blood. While Dwight and I did not understand all the medical jargon, we knew it was very serious. Standard chemotherapy protocol was prescribed and started that night.

A porta-cath would be surgically implanted just under the skin to access lines carrying strong drugs into her body with hopes of fighting and eradicating the cancer.

As only the Lord could have planned it, Anna's only St. Louis friend, Mr. Brasfield, who had just two days ago been our houseguest in Paris, now sat on the edge of her hospital bed explaining how his own porta-cath worked. He showed it to her and helped her understand why it was important for her treatment. Anna could not have had a better friend than Earl Brasfield. He also befriended Josh and Jonathan during Anna's hospitalization, taking them to his farm for swimming in the creek and other "guy fun." He faithfully prayed and encouraged through many months.

Scheduled to surgically implant the porta-cath, Dr. Mike Skinner came to Anna's room to meet her and explain the procedure. This fine young surgeon shared his faith and offered to pray. His prayer for us that day was like a balm to our trembling souls. We would never forget it.

Flowers, stuffed animals, snacks, and other loving gifts poured into Anna's hospital room. Every Wednesday a different funny card arrived from Mr. Boothe in Texas. How in the world did Mrs. Polly manage to find so many? But she did.

Rick Draehn's Sunday School class at Parkway, Dwight's new church, sent a journal signed by members of the class with notes of encouragement. The journal was meant for Anna, but she resisted the idea of writing about her challenge, saying she didn't want to remember any of this. I asked Anna if she would like for me to write in the journal, to record the days for her. If she wanted it later, it would be there; if not, that would be O.K. too. That pleased her, and so began the chronicle.

On Saturday there was a knock at the door, and there stood Anna's best friend, Beth Ann, with Mama Sue and Dr. Mel. What a surprise and joyful reunion for those two. Anna was so thrilled to see her precious Bethie. The nurses let us take her in a wheelchair with accompanying IV pole down to the atrium for ice cream. It was fun and encouraging, more than well worth the exhaustion and violent sickness that followed.

For several days chemo seemed to reign; she could not keep anything down. Even chicken broth came back up. One day she said, "Would you please ask Daddy to stop at Taco Bell and bring me a tostada?"

Her nurses and I were concerned, but we relayed the request. Our hero Dad brought in the familiar savory paper sack with her special order. Anna ate almost all and kept it down. The child was a true Texan.

After the first round of chemo, Anna was released for a few days. Her "big sister" and former baby sitter Amy Blakeman flew in, to Anna's delight. They talked and giggled and hugged for two days. Later, Amy's mother Sharon relayed what Anna had shared with Amy—that she knew she might die and that really was okay. Anna's greatest concern was how much that would hurt her Mom.

Friday, June 16, as Anna and I drove to Children's Hospital for our scheduled out-patient visit, we chatted about the beautiful morning and what we might like for lunch. At the hospital we were almost immediately separated, and I was soon surrounded by members of the medical team. They explained that the chemo had not been effective, that it had not lessened at all the leukemia cells in her bone marrow. Anna's condition was grave. I became nauseous while listening and muttered, "Excuse me, I think I'm sick," and woke up later on a cot. They called and told Dwight that I had fainted and he came to the hospital.

Anna was still occupied in visiting with her hospital friends while we listened to the rest of the report.

The doctors gave her little hope, ten to fifteen percent or less. There was a rare combination of problems with ALL–Philadelphia Chromosome and Monosomy 7 present. Harder chemo could be devastating. One option was to keep Anna at home with no further treatment. When Dwight asked how long she would have with that option, they guessed about two weeks. We said "no," that we would not give up.

When Anna was ushered in to join us, she walked over to share my upholstered chair in a tight squeeze. I explained to her that the leukemia was more difficult than we had at first thought and that she would need even harder treatments. Was she up for it?

She responded typically, "Whatever you think."

It was a hard weekend. Bittersweet. Lots of laughter, lots of private tears. My crying place was in the shower. I was the cleanest person in America.

When the Bible says to "Pray without ceasing," that weekend comes to mind–there was constant, incessant, desperate prayer. I determined before the Lord to concentrate on Him and on Anna, not on the disease.

Anna is alive, and as long as there is breath in her body we will focus on life and hope. I refuse to bury her now. I hope she lives to old age and buries me first. At any rate, I refuse to spend the days, weeks, months to come feeling sorry for myself at the possibility of losing her. I am certainly weak, but the Lord is strong. 'In my weakness His strength is made perfect.' Anna needs a strong mother, not a whiner.

It was a mantra often repeated in the following months. We would not waste one precious day of her life on "what ifs." Every day we were together would be a celebration of her life. If and when the time came to grieve, I certainly would, but not until then. At least, this was my heart's intent. Then, there were the inevitable leaky tear ducts. Back to the shower.

On Monday we again checked into Children's Hospital to begin a chemo combination of two very hard drugs with warnings to expect horrible side effects. Because of low counts, Anna was in an isolation room right across from the nurses' station. Nurses and the new summer crop of interns gave her a sense of community even in isolation as they came to visit as well as to provide assigned care.

Anna's room overlooked Forest Park, where the famed outdoor Municipal Opera, "The Muny," held nightly performances. Since the hospital was behind the stage area, we could only see light coming from around the trees and lines of cars winding through the park. During one week, every evening about nine-thirty, fireworks would shoot up from the Muny. Nurses told us it was the scene in "Cinderella" when she marries the prince and lives happily ever after. I promised Anna we would take her to the Muny as soon as she was well.

On the Fourth of July, Anna was too weak to ride down the hall to observe the spectacular fireworks from the St. Louis Arch. However, we were pleasantly surprised that from her bed she could see distant fireworks displays from smaller townships. It was another small blessing.

One special visit was allowed during this time. Mary Engelbreit, a St. Louis artist whose work Anna had admired in Texas, came in after receiving a telephone call from one of the nurses. She brought a bag full of goodies and a kind, quiet spirit that immediately drew Anna and Dwight and me to her. Anna was suddenly shy but noted Mary's dangly earrings, tiny painted watering cans. "Oooh," she softly crooned. "They look like Mary Engelbreit."

The obvious response, "They are."

Mary became Anna's special friend and encourager, as dear a person as her famous illustrations suggest.

As predicted, the chemo was awful and related treatments were even worse.

Amphotericin (Ampho-terrible) was one of the worst—rigors that rocked the bed, nausea with retching, then sweats. Anna's nurse had to remain in the room while the IV ran and take vitals every ten minutes. This was strong poison. Horrible. One night Dwight balked at the medication, and Anna explained to him that it was necessary and she had to have it. It was an interesting role reversal.

The Ampho had to continue until her counts came back—A.N.C., absolute neutrophil count. When Anna wanted spicy beef jerky, Dwight found some. She loved the jerky and shared it with medical personnel. We also had tortilla chips and hot sauce one night. Dr. Rob Hanson posted a hand-made sign on her door: "Please feed the neutrophils. Salsa. Must be HOT."

Saturday, July 15, her counts started coming back. We could stop the Amphotericin. Thank You, Lord. The A.N.C. count rose dramatically. We called it "Anna's Neutrophil Count." Saturday 32, Sunday 100, Monday 350.

The third bone marrow test showed that although Anna was not in remission, only about nine percent leukemia cells were evident as compared to 70 to 80 percent in previous tests. A bone marrow transplant was one possibility but a very long shot and not available at Children's Hospital's three-bed unit. Dr. John Dipersio, Chief of Bone Marrow Transplant at Barnes Hospital, agreed to consider Anna as a possible transplant candidate. He would study her case and then interview her and our family.

From the journal:

We know that Anna belongs to God and we have already given her back to Him. He loves her with a greater love than is humanly possible for us, and we can trust Him to take care of her. We implored the Lord for the life of our dear child.

Dwight, Joshua, Jonathan, and I were all typed to see if one of us might be Anna's bone marrow donor. Dr. Ed Horowitz performed the DNA studies and excitedly reported to us that Josh was a match! It was a 5/6 match, the one mismatch being the least important. He would take Josh at 5/6 before a 6/6 non-family member.

On Anna's last day at Children's Hospital, in trooped all the interns and residents with an ice cream cake inscribed "We love you, Anna." What a touching scene. We learned that Dr. Rob Hanson had actually bought the cake and organized the surprise.

Dwight's mother lived south of St. Louis about forty minutes away, so we had a family week together at Grandmother's house. It was wonderful. We set up a twin bed in the small parlor off the family room and I slept next to Anna on the sofa. Home health care brought out IV paraphernalia, medicines, and a refrigerator for TPN bags. Nurses taught me the morning, afternoon, and evening regimens and we got along.

Josh and Jonathan loved having their sister with them. They spent hours in her room. Jonathan even brought his sleeping bag down one night and slept on the floor.

The boys helped create menus for meals, and I would go to the grocery store between IV's while they visited with their sister. When she felt strong enough, we took her out for a movie matinee and another time for some quick shopping. What a special time.

July 25 was Anna's appointment with Dr. Dipersio, who received all five of us as a family venture. He seemed positive and encouraging about stem cell therapy, Josh's donor match, and the graft versus host disease advantage in this case because the match was 5/6. His hope was that Josh's burly cells would gobble up any of Anna's remaining leukemia cells. Barnes Hospital and its special Bone Marrow Transplant Unit was designed for adult patients only. As chief of the service, Dr. Dipersio was willing to make an exception for thirteen-year-old Anna and to accept her as his personal patient. Did Anna understand that? Was she willing to go through the arduous transplant process in an all adult environment?

She answered, "Yessir," and the rest of us thanked him sincerely.

We returned to Grandmother's house encouraged and very aware of the serious challenge before us. Ahead loomed a huge mountain for Anna and also for Joshua as her donor. We prepared for the long "siege" in the hospital's transplant unit with books and other suggested items. Goodie bags for Joshua's three days of pheresis contained movie videos and snacks. In the few remaining days before the transplant process, we intentionally made happy family memories. Only the Lord knew what the outcome would be.

The next day from upstairs at Grandmother's house, I heard the front door click.

Looking out the window, I saw Anna standing out on the grassy side lawn, pale, thin, with short wispy strands of red hair still shimmering in the sun. She was alone. What thoughts were going through her mind as she stood there all by herself?

She slowly, deliberately made her way into the yard, a beautiful valley just beyond the end of the gravel road. I stood at the window and looked down at my precious beloved child, now frail and sick but still strong in spirit. How could such purity and goodness be embraced in one little girl?

I recalled the story Jesus told about a woman who kept knocking and knocking and knocking on the judge's door until finally he gave in and granted her request. Jesus said He told the parable "to show that at all times they ought to pray and not to lose heart" (Luke 18:1). In the parable Jesus was demonstrating only one principle: persistence.

As I looked out from that second-floor window to the meadow below and the child of my heart, I whispered, "Lord, *please* heal her." Then again, "Please heal her; please heal her; please heal her."

The chest of drawers stood next to the window. I knocked on the top of that wood furniture with knuckles bent to purpose. I knocked again and again. Tears streamed down my face as I implored Him: "Lord, I'm knocking. Can you hear me? I'm knocking and knocking and knocking."

Please heal Anna.

Darryl and Ginnie Wikoff gave us tickets for the Cardinals/ Cubs game on Saturday. We usually reserved Saturday evenings for Sunday preparation, but the children had never been to a Cubs game and Anna especially wanted to go. Dwight and I didn't see how she could manage it physically but agreed that if she felt like it, we would try.

One of her strong motivations was that Todd Zeile, recently traded by St. Louis to Chicago, would be returning to Busch Stadium for the first time. Anna sensed this return might be hard and potentially embarrassing for Zeile, and she felt compelled to somehow convey to him that someone in St. Louis still remembered him kindly. She sent me to Wal-Mart for bright yellow poster board; then she labored with colored markers to carefully print a sign: "We Miss You, Todd! Good luck with the Cubbies!"

Anna spent most of Saturday in bed with a very sick tummy, but quietly dressed in her red Cardinal shirt as the afternoon waned. Earlier we had unpacked a box from Texas containing her track shoes, and after they were washed and dried, she had pulled them to her and kissed them. She wore them now.

We packed a tote bag of medicine and other necessities and loaded up in the Mama Bus. As we crunched down the gravel lane, Anna reclined back in the seat, all her energy expended on preparation to go to the game.

At the stadium, Dwight pulled up to the gate nearest our seats in the ground floor section. Anna would not have to climb. She slowly walked all the way, refusing a wheelchair. Our seats were good, near the front at the third base line. Soon after we were seated, some of the players started practicing out on the field, and then came Todd Zeile to warm up. When the children caught sight of him, they held up the sign, but no response indicated that he had seen it. They waited for him to turn in their direction again—up went the sign. No response.

Anna got to her feet and slowly, precariously started down the aisle steps toward the railed edge. Jonathan took her arm and went, too. They held up the sign. Zeile saw it and flashed a warm smile and wave with a "Thank you."

That was all it took. The beaming little girl with red wisps peeking out from under her baseball cap laboriously made her way back to her seat, cheeks flushed and eyes shining. "Oh, Mom!" she softly exclaimed. "He saw it! Did you see his face? He saw it and he knew that somebody cared about him."

Her mission complete, she settled into the molded stadium seat like a limp rag doll with an expression of utter contentment and satisfaction. Looking at her angelic smile and sweet countenance, I thought how typical this episode was. Her emphasis had nothing to do with herself. There was only one purpose here, to bring joy to someone else; and in so doing, she was happy herself.

The usher for our section came over and asked if she would like him to take the sign down to the dug-out, understanding that she would not get it back. Anna was thrilled. She wrote and signed a note on the back and off it went, she knew, to the person she had hoped to bless.

A few minutes later she became ill and had to leave. Dwight drove Anna and me home, allowing the boys to stay and watch the game. Even as we got into the car and she was violently sick, Anna still had a small light in her eyes and said again, "He saw it. He knows."

Sunday morning the guys went to Parkway, Grandmother went to church and lunch with friends, and after morning health care rituals Anna lay on the couch as we had "church." We read Philippians 4 and then sang her favorite hymns and camp songs, including "Only Trust Him."

> Come every soul by sin oppressed, there's mercy with the Lord;
>
> And He will surely give you rest by trusting in His Word.
>
> Only trust Him, only trust Him, only trust Him now.
>
> He will save you, He will save you, He will save you now.
>
> Yes, Jesus is the truth, the way that leads you into rest.
>
> Believe in Him without delay and you are fully blessed.

We sang with fervor and then our prayer time was tender. I knelt next to her couch and we held hands as we each offered the Lord thanks for His goodness. The very second we got to ". . . in Jesus' name. . ." the phone rang. A hasty "Amen," three steps to the telephone, and a man's voice asked if this might be the residence of Anna Blankenship and could he speak to her.

It was someone from Busch Stadium. Anna took the receiver, listened, and glowed. "Oh, yes. No problem. My Dad will come right down this afternoon."

The man was telling her that a baseball had been left in the office personally inscribed to Anna from Todd Zeile with the message, "Thanks for the support!"

Needless to say, Dwight and the boys were dispatched with haste to the stadium after church. They got to see a few innings for free, and Anna had a reminder that happiness given away always comes back.

HOPE

A week of total body irradiation and another week of cranial radiation were ordered to "bomb" Anna's body with her maximum lifetime quotient of radiation. Hopefully any lurking cancer cells would be eradicated before the stem cell transplant. From her corner room in the bone marrow transplant unit of Barnes Hospital on the thirteenth floor of Queeny Tower, spacious windows all across the front wall overlooked beautiful Forest Park.

Apple green letters on a deep purple background boldly spelled out Philippians 4:13, the promise banner Sharon Foster had mailed to Anna while at Children's Hospital. "I can do all things through Christ who strengthens me."

We copied many other verses of hope on brightly colored paper and taped them to otherwise white walls. Framed photos of Anna with her brothers, friends, and Sweet Granny cheered the room along with balloons, posters, and gift packages. Flowers were not allowed on the bone marrow unit.

Mr. Jarrell, one of Anna's teachers from Bailey Middle School in Texas, mailed Anna a photograph he had taken of her for the school yearbook just before running in a track meet. Unaware of the camera, Anna stood in profile, her thick red ponytail shining under the bright Texas sky as she looked intently ahead toward the goal. The snapshot was taken only weeks before her diagnosis, still out there giving it her best even as this hideous disease secretly began wreaking havoc in her young body. Mr. Jarrell had the picture enlarged to a poster that daily inspired us.

We adopted some "rules" gleaned from the good counsel of several encouragers.

- Read Scripture aloud. This was a mainstay for us.
- Touch a lot. Anna needed to feel my presence physically and I needed hers, too.
- Laugh. We tried to find at least one funny thing each day to laugh about. Usually that was not difficult for us, but on days that it was, we pulled out her Aggie Joke Book or watched "America's Funniest Home Videos." Proverbs says, "A merry heart does good like medicine."
- Eat well. Junk food from the machines were replaced by fruits and veggies, within parameters of BMT protocol.

Sunday, August 13, Anna and I had church. We read in Mark 7 about the deaf and mute man who was healed by Jesus.

From the journal:

It wasn't like some of the other healings. Jesus, instead of just speaking a word, "took the man aside from the multitude by himself, and put His fingers in his ears, and after spitting, He touched his tongue with the saliva; and looking up to Heaven with a deep sigh, He said to him. . . 'Be opened.' And his ears were opened, and the impediment of his tongue was removed, and he began speaking plainly."

Perhaps the reason Jesus didn't heal the man instantly with a word was because the step-by-step process was vital to the man's spiritual as well as physical experience.

Because he couldn't hear, Jesus used simple action pictures to help him understand the progression of the healing–

> took him aside by himself;
>
> put His fingers in his ears;
>
> spit, then touched the man's tongue with His saliva (Genesis 2:7, He had breathed into Adam's nostrils the breath of life);
>
> looked up to Heaven (His source of power);
>
> sighed (perhaps because the man would now face life's hardest temptation to sin, the tongue, James 3); and only then
>
> gave the verbal command, "Be opened."

The first step is particularly significant, because when Jesus took the deaf/mute man aside by himself, he was able to focus only on Jesus without the distraction of other people and their needs. I can almost feel his wonder. The first audible voice he ever heard was that of Jesus.

I wonder if these months of Anna's illness are part of God's plan to re-work the ears and mouth of Sherry Ann, her mama. As we spend day after day in isolation, it is easier for Him to have my undivided attention, to focus on the truths of His Word, to hear only Him.

Lord, keep the voices of the "multitude" subdued so I can listen clearly to You. My tongue needs taming. Please use this time for good. Teach me discipline and wisdom, "the law of kindness" (Proverbs 31). That would certainly be one of the good things You could bring from this terrible situation.

Anna's mouth and throat hurt badly and she couldn't sing, so I sang our old faithful hymn alone; but she began to mouth the words and then whisper them as I sang. Only the Lord and Anna could ever enjoy my singing.

How firm a foundation, ye saints of the Lord

Is laid for your faith in His excellent Word.

What more can we say than to you He hath said

To you who for refuge to Jesus have fled?

"Fear not, I am with thee; oh, be not dismayed

For I am thy God and will still give thee aid.

I'll strengthen thee, help thee, and cause thee to stand,

Upheld by My righteous, omnipotent hand.

"When through fiery trials thy pathway shall lie,

My grace all-sufficient shall be thy supply.

The flame shall not hurt thee; I only design

Thy dross to consume and thy gold to refine.

"The soul that on Jesus hath leaned for repose,

I will not, I will not desert to its foes.

That soul, though all hell should endeavor to shake,

I'll never, no never, no never forsake."

My voice quivered on the final notes, and the tears in Anna's eyes reflected my own.

"It's true," I managed to say. "Satan's tried to shake us."

She nodded, the tears now rolling down her cheeks–mine, too.

I added, "But he can't, can he?"

Anna shook her head in response, "Because the Lord's gonna kick him in the teeth."

That afternoon Anna had visitors, Dr. Janet Mueller and Dr. Rob Hanson. She was delighted. After initial hugs and greetings, Janet produced binoculars with instructions to look across the expanse of several city blocks to Children's Hospital, the corner window of ninth floor. We could see a large white sign in the window, but couldn't quite make out its letters. With binoculars the message was clear for all the world to see: WE LOVE YOU ANNA!

How dear of them. Anna was tickled to her toes. She laughed and talked and we saw the old Anna again. The exertion was a bit much, and when they left she was very sick, but that definitely made a "keeper" memory.

From the journal:

It's late Monday evening. Anna has been very sick today but consistently refused medication that would make her sleepy. We begged her to please take some pain medicine. She finally consented, and after two shots of morphine was able to drift off to sleep. Her peaceful rest now is a blessing. Her angel face lies on a pretty pillowcase Venna sent her, and there is no evidence of the physical torture she has been enduring.

Tomorrow is the big day, the transplant. Joshua is to begin pheresis at 7:30 AM. Lord, please give him courage and grace to endure for those six hours. Bless his veins to be strong enough and his cells mean enough to deliver Your healing to his sister. In the name of Jesus, by whose stripes we are healed, kill absolutely any remaining vestige of the leukemia and bring new life to the marrow of Anna's bones through the great gift of her brother.

August 15—Transplant Day. Anna, though very sick in the morning, was only concerned for Joshua, strapped into a pheresis recliner in a nearby building of the sprawling medical center. As much for Anna as myself, I slipped away long enough to quickly walk the maze of linking walkways to our precious boy.

He was taking it like a man, tubes and needles inserted in his right arm and back of his left hand, required to be absolutely motionless for the whole day, no small feat for this active thirteen-year-old. Dwight and Jonathan fed him and took care of every other need. Joshua showed such great love and courage in this immense gift to his sister, which also included painful neuprogen injections for days before the transplant and long additional pheresis sessions after the transplant for granulacytes, premature white blood cells to help Anna fight infection during neutropenic days.

The writer of Ecclesiastes could not have put it better: "A cord of three strands is not easily broken." These three young people, conceived together in one womb, held an unmistakable bond.

From the journal:

When Jonathan got a head injury on the playground at school this spring, Anna had a terrible pain in her head in another classroom. During her first chemo treatments at Children's Hospital she became really sick with nausea and vomiting. The next morning Dwight told us Josh would not be able to visit Anna that day because he had been throwing up during the night. Josh has even asked if he can shave his head when the last sparse wisps of Anna's hair come out. (Mama's has already been coming out right along with Anna's.)

The only time Anna cried when we were at Children's (besides the bone marrow tests) was when they explained the transplant process and she learned that Josh would need injections, blood draws, and pheresis.

"Just *please* don't stick him," she begged. "There's got to be another way to do it so you don't have to stick him. He hates that. You just don't understand."

Barb Tesno asked Anna, "If Josh needed a transplant, would you do this for him?"

Anna nodded.

Barb continued, "Then don't deny him this opportunity to do it for you."

Not long before school's end in May, the children studied genetics in science. Their teacher used these three as an example of multiple births, and in Jonathan's class she asked him some direct questions related to being a triplet. One classmate raised his hand and directed a question to Jonathan.

"So, when Josh gets hurt, do you feel it?"

Jonathan's reply: "Only if I hit him."

From the journal:

WEDNESDAY, AUGUST 16–DAY 1
The transplant staff refers to preparatory days as -3, -2, -1. The actual day of transplant is Day 0, and the day after begins Day 1.

"I love the Lord because He has heard my voice and my supplications. Because He has inclined His ear to me, therefore I will call upon Him as long as I live." Psalm 116:1–2.

Yesterday went without a hitch. The Lord gave us a wonderful experience as a family. Not only did Joshua have enough stem cells (there was some concern because of his youth), but two-and-a-half times more than was required, and Anna got them all. We held hands around her bed and Dwight prayed that they would find "home" in her bones and that God would use them to give her new life.

Later she asked for nausea and pain medication, and after a couple of shots of morphine she slept peacefully until into the wee hours of the morning.

Dr. Dipersio came by. Anna was asleep so we talked in the hall. He noted the Texas A&M shirt she was wearing for the transplant and pointed to her A&M sticker he still wears on his nametag, despite great harassment from Washington University colleagues. He candidly answered some tough questions and I was encouraged. We do not dwell on "odds," but it was good to hear his were twenty per cent.

For Anna, the stem cell transplant itself seemed pretty unremarkable after all her other treatments. Nurse Jane hung a bag of IV fluid containing life-giving stem cells extracted from Joshua's blood from the pole by her hospital bed, and that was it. Those stem cells from Joshua would find their way into Anna's bone marrow where they were supposed to go. There they would duke it out with her cells to see who would be boss—"graft (Josh's cells) versus host (Anna's cells) disease," and, as Dr. Dipersio had predicted, Anna's GVH was horrendous.

In the weeks following transplant, Anna's skin, tissues, even her fingernails and toenails were replaced by new tissue. Her skin peeled like a burn victim, very painful in addition to severe nausea that persisted. It looked awful. In the beginning she also endured tissue breakdown caused by the enormous bombard-ment of chemo and radiation in preparation for the transplant.

Anna's young intern friends from Children's Hospital, espe-cially Dr. Janet Kao and Dr. Lori Kutka, and many of her former nurses trekked over the walkway network to Barnes Hospital almost every day. Her primary care nurse, Shelly Fleuchel, even created matching bright yellow tee-shirts for Anna and herself.

Our new Parkway Baptist family prayed around the clock and sent dinners for every evening to Grandmother's house.

Dr. Jim Fleshman, Dwight's deacon and the boys' Sunday School teacher, came each afternoon to see Anna, always seem-ing to pop in exactly when his expertise and encouragement were most needed.

White-haired Beatty Miller, a Parkway senior adult, several times sent his special Juicy Fruit chewing gum, which Anna enthusiastically unwrapped. Mr. Miller's "gum" was carefully replaced with a folded dollar bill. Sundays when Dwight arrived at the hospital after church, she would eagerly ask, "Did you bring me some chewing gum?" We were blessed with kind sup-port from every direction.

During those weeks Anna and I memorized this nugget from Philippians 4:

> "Rejoice in the Lord always, and again I say, rejoice.

> "Let your forbearing spirit be known to all men; the Lord is near.

> "Be anxious for nothing, but in everything by prayer and supplication with thanksgiving let your requests be made known to God.

"And the peace which passes all understanding shall guard your hearts and minds in Christ Jesus.

"Finally, brethren, whatever is true, whatever is honorable, whatever is right, whatever is pure, whatever is lovely, whatever is of good repute, if there is any excellence and if anything worthy of praise, let your mind dwell on these things.

"The things you have learned and received and heard and seen in me, practice these things; and the God of peace shall be with you.

"I have learned to be content in whatsoever state I am.

"I know how to get along with humble means, and I also know how to live in prosperity; in any and every circumstance, I have learned the secret of being filled and going hungry, both of having abundance and suffering need.

"I can do all things through Christ who strengthens me.

"My God shall supply all your needs according to His riches in glory in Christ Jesus."

Verses were memorized and added one at a time over days and weeks in the transplant room. At night as Anna and I lay in the semi-darkness, one of us would begin, "Rejoice . . ." and the other would chime in and we would say the verses together.

Anna's gentle spirit never wavered through the long, grueling transplant ordeal. One day her nurse said, "Anna, there are men on this hall who can't take the pain you do. It's O.K. for you to yell and scream!" to which Anna smiled and remained her dear self.

The journal records an incident when I walked to the door-way of her room from doing our laundry down the hall of the self-contained transplant unit. Dr. Dipersio was at her bedside talking to her. He asked if there was anything she wanted.

"What do you mean?" she asked.

Dr.: "Money, a boat, a car. *Anything.*"

Anna: "You could let me stop the mouth washes."

Dr.: "Mmmm. . . (shaking his head). . . can't do that."

We did our best to make Anna's hospital room feel like "home," and the best part of that were visits from Dwight and Josh and Jonathan. We had learned all too well that "home" is not a "house." Home is where the heart is, and ours was in Anna's hospital room. Josh and Jonathan usually came on Friday eve-nings after school and on Sundays after church. The love in that room could have warmed the whole world.

One of our favorite gifts was Ron Mehl's *God Works the Night Shift.* When Dwight was able to come in the evenings, Anna and I would ask him to read a chapter aloud to us. As soon as he finished the book, we asked him to start over and read it to us again.

During this period Channel 5, the NBC television affili-ate in St. Louis, called asking to interview Anna and our family. After their first story they returned twice more in response to viewer contacts about Anna's progress and a fourth word the following year. We were surprised and grateful for this encour-agement that prompted many people we did not know to pray for Anna.

If Anna were writing this herself, I know she would say the high point of this time was her friend Dr. Rob Hanson's deci-sion to commit his life to Jesus Christ. It was glorious. Dr. Rob deliberately waited for baptism until the following Spring when

Anna was well enough to come, too. We slipped her into church in a wheelchair with a face mask to see her Daddy baptize her wonderful doctor, a brilliant man of science who had come to know that Christ was real through the simple witness of one young patient.

From the journal, August 22:

A Mickey Mouse mylar balloon caught my eye this afternoon on its way up and away. The face and ears of Mickey were far above our thirteenth floor window as it kept climbing and drifting. I wondered where it would land. Thank You, Lord, for the security of knowing we are not adrift, but securely in Your care.

QUESTIONS

Anna pleaded to be released from the hospital for her birthday, and Dr. Dipersio and his team reluctantly agreed. Despite withering weakness and ongoing gastric symptoms of raging graft versus host disease, Anna was overjoyed to be "home" at Grandmother's house with Josh and Jonathan for their shared birthday. With discharge came home orders for five IV medications on three different pumps and thirty-three pills a day. As Anna and I were driving away from the pharmacy service window one day, we thanked God for insurance. She tried to eat, but only nibbles were possible, even of her favorites.

September 24, 1995, the children's fourteenth birthday, landed on Sunday. Anna's only request was to attend church at Parkway. Her doctors agreed if we arrived after morning worship began and left during the final prayer to minimize risk of exposure to infection. That afternoon Josh and Jonathan enjoyed the St. Louis Rams/Chicago Bears football game while Anna slept (with IV's), exhausted but happy.

On Saturday, Beth Ann and Sue Young flew up to see Anna and back to Texas the same afternoon, a precious gift. Anna lay on the couch as Bethie played her flute. They smiled and even giggled a little, but the melancholy air was unmistakable as they expressed love for one another and held each other tightly. It pulled my heartstrings.

Texas A&M gifts continued to pour in—a football signed by each of the current football players with a personal note to Anna on it from coach R. C. Slocum, special A&M athletic shoes, tee-shirts, caps, socks, even taped music of the A&M men's choir.

Anna smiled at each one, further cementing her allegiance to the Aggies.

Make A Wish Foundation called more than once asking Anna to request a special gift, but she could not think of anything to request, each time deferring to other children who might not have so much as she. At last, with their prodding, she asked for a computer, knowing it would be a great treat for her brothers. She patiently lay in her twin bed in the parlor as kind Make A Wish folks set up the computer in the only tiny space on the opposite wall. Joshua took to it immediately, and Anna delighted in watching the obvious excitement and joy it brought to both brothers and her adoring Daddy.

Because it was important to Anna that she keep up with her brothers and graduate together in the year 2000, a homebound teacher was assigned by the school district to help her catch up on schoolwork. Anna already had some creative ideas about a custom designed high school graduation card, "The Last Thing We Will Do Together." With "Miss Linda" Ray she was able to study English, math, history, and science, and was even inducted into the National Junior Honor Society.

Steroids seemed to help increase Anna's appetite, but the perpetual upset tummy from graft versus host made it impossible to regain strength. Her weight continued to drop, once twelve pounds in two weeks. We were up several times every night with IV pumps and sick tummy. She became so weak we could only walk with me behind her, my arms circled under her arms holding on. Through it all, she never complained.

From the journal:

Anna is very weak and tired. She lays on the couch all day except to go to the bathroom or for our little outings to the post office or drive-through pharmacy. She cannot step up to the front door without assistance and great effort. The steroids give her 'chipmunk cheeks' which make her self-conscious. She is an angel. She never complains or whines. She has always been a dear, sweet child, but there is a grace in her spirit now that runs deep. She says very little but manifests the love and peace of Jesus profoundly.

The journal is full of prayers and scripture readings. It was only the faithful, everlasting arms of God that sustained us in those days. I sensed Anna's life slipping away and felt helpless to stop the slide. We just trusted the Lord and kept plugging away.

We talked with her doctors by phone often and went in for regular clinic checks. Sometimes they expressed need for Anna's return to the hospital, but she begged to remain at home with her brothers, so we would try again with tweaked treatment regimens. Prolonged TPN use affected her sugar levels, which now also required finger pricks and insulin shots, the worst part of Anna's care for me. My eyes would tear up before a shot, and Anna would comfort me, saying it really didn't hurt very much.

Monday, October 23, the journal records an incident that was a life marker. After supper I had taken muffins to the freezer in the basement and "happened" to glimpse a snatch of color out the basement window. A closer look revealed the bright purple jigsaw piece of a beautiful rainbow! I ran upstairs and out the front door. There, grandly arching above the treetops and down to earth on both sides was the most perfect, vivid rainbow I had ever seen. I called the children to come quickly. Even Anna made her way gingerly the few steps to the door to behold the wonder. We snapped pictures of it; in only minutes it had disappeared.

From the journal:

It's a promise—God's symbol of hope to mankind dwelling in a sinful, grossly imperfect world. It is a simple pictorial reminder in our horribly complicated human existence. Had I remained intent on my own pursuit down in the basement, I would have missed it. I had to look *up*. How many others of God's wonders have I missed while looking down in preoccupation?

Several years ago I came across Revelation 4:3 that says God's throne in heaven is encircled by a "multi-colored bow." Genesis 9 is the account of God's promise after the flood. I had always thought God made a rainbow and put it up in the sky as a sign of His promise never to destroy the earth again by water. A closer examination of Genesis 9:13 was clear: "I set *My bow* in the cloud, and it shall be for a sign of a covenant between Me and the earth."

God didn't make a rainbow as a sign of promise. He set *His* bow in the sky as His signature on the promise. I could only see half of the bow tonight—the earth was in the way. If I could have seen it from Heaven, it would have been a full circle with the world out of the way.

Oh, Father, prompt me to look up, to be watching for You. Lift my gaze above the troubles of this world to behold Your glory. Thank You, Master, Creator, and Sovereign Lord, for the sign of promise tonight. When Ezekiel (1:28) saw Your glory, he compared it to a rainbow. Thank You for allowing me a glimpse of Your majesty in the twilight sky. Thine is the kingdom and the power and the glory forever. Amen.

When Anna and I lay down later with lights dimmed, we talked about seeing the beautiful rainbow. What would it be like to view it from Heaven, encircling God's throne like a giant multi-colored hula-hoop?

Unless Jesus came back first, one of us would be going to heaven before the other one. We agreed that night that our special signal if and when that time came, would be the rainbow. If the one of us in Heaven saw God pick up His bow and wave it for people on earth to see, we would know that the other one remembered two promises: first, that He would never again destroy the earth by water, and, for us, that we would be together someday in Heaven. A promise is a promise, we agreed, as both of us wept. I never forgot, and I'm sure neither did she.

The following days had little ups and downs, but Anna was basically so weak she could hardly move in bed, much less sit or stand alone. Through it all she remained sweet to the core. She fell a couple of times, even with us helping her.

From the journal:

Her little legs just give way sometimes. In the middle of the night she woke me suddenly. "Mom—we forgot something!"

"What???"

"We forgot to thank God that I was not seriously hurt today."

She was right, so at 3:00 AM or so, I knelt in the darkness by her bed as she thanked God in prayer.

The Aunts called during that same week to share with us the necessity for Sweet Granny to be moved into a skilled nursing facility. She had been with Aunt Elaine for several months after she was no longer able to live in her white farmhouse on the hill that had been home for more than seventy years. While we recognized the loving necessity of this decision, it was also starkly apparent that life would never be the same for Granny or for us.

This touched an especially tender point for Anna. Our kind Aunts sent photographs to her of Granny in her pretty new room and even held the phone to her ear for Anna to talk. With quiet grace Anna acknowledged it all and continued to pray daily for her dear great-grandmother.

We seemed to be very near the valley of the shadow. Anna weighed less than a hundred pounds fully clothed with shoes. She was strangely yellow and weak, but very aware and determined to carry on. One evening she shared that she knew Heaven would be wonderful and she really was ready to go, but she had always thought Jesus was coming to get us, and our family would all go together. She never wanted to go by herself. Surely, she pondered, God would not want to mess up our family, would He?

We talked about the valley of the shadow of death, what that description might mean. We decided that death, which seemed real to us, was really only a "shadow."

It seemed scary to us, but when we got to the valley we would not be afraid because Jesus would meet us there and walk us over to the other side. "Yea, though I walk through the valley of the shadow of death, I will fear no evil, for Thou art with me."

These conversations usually took place after prayers and "lights out." I would probably not have initiated them; but when Anna did, she could freely express her feelings and I tried to go with her. It would have been much easier to avoid the subject of death—a la "protecting" her and thus protecting my own raw pain at the possibility of losing her. But when it was on her mind, she could and did bring it up with honest candor. Otherwise, we concentrated on life in the present moment. I was and am glad that she felt free to share at least some of the things she was thinking and feeling.

From the journal:

Bedtime came late and for some reason Anna and I had prayer time alone. As I knelt by her bedside, she prayed, thanking God for specifics and interceding by name for a list of those she regularly lifts to Him. My prayer included thanks for the assurance that one day all five of us will be in Heaven with Him for eternity because of what Jesus has done for us. Anna softly agreed, "Me too, Lord."

After the "Amen" she told me she thinks about Heaven often and looks forward to the day we are all there together with Jesus.

"Just think, Mom. Everything will be perfect, none of the junk of this world." She talked about perfect peace and rest. Her face and eyes were shining with genuine assurance of what the Bible calls "the blessed hope."

Later as I lay under covers on the couch in the darkness, tears rolled down my cheeks unabated at the crystal clear realization that my prayers and efforts to hold Anna here on earth with me are utterly selfish. The joy of Heaven awaits her in Jesus, and I daily plead with Him to leave her here. I tried again to relinquish that hold to Him but do not find it easy.

Hard as they were, maybe those discussions made our joy and affection even more genuine. We seemed to draw strength from one another as we leaned together on the Lord's strong arms.

One night Anna dreamed we were at Granny's white farmhouse. The next morning she asked if Heaven might be sort of like Granny's house. It certainly wasn't a "mansion" in worldly terms, but the presence of Jesus was real there and it sure was beautiful to us. Maybe so, baby girl.

Thursday, November 9, after supper dishes and between IV's, I was helping Anna with her bath when she became increasingly unresponsive. Dwight came in and helped with dressing and getting her to the couch. She had a blank faraway look in her eyes and did not respond to my questions. As I started to call the doctor she began to jerk violently and eyes rolled back in her head. Dwight did CPR as I dialed 911.

The 911 operator talked us through the terrifying minutes that followed. Blood from the mouth; she had bit her tongue. No response. Blue. It seemed like an eternity. The operator said to click the front porch light on and off as a signal for the ambulance while she stayed on the phone. Panic froze like ice in my veins as Dwight continued CPR and I watched and clicked and kept repeating, "Please, hurry."

Sirens wailing, ambulance lights soon appeared coming down the gravel road. Skilled paramedics were efficient, strong, and kind. God bless them. They tended to Anna, who was now awake, with compassion and competence, then allowed me to ride with them to Barnes Hospital as Dwight followed close behind.

In the emergency room, a CT scan showed some unusual spots on the brain. An MRI the next day confirmed the presence of lesions. Dr. Dipersio and his medical team called in a neurologist and also Dr. Dacy, lead neurosurgeon, who would perform a biopsy on the top lesion on Monday. That night

Anna prayed from her hospital bed, "Lord, thank you for Your peace that passes our understanding."

Sunday afternoon another seizure gripped Anna, longer than the previous one. "Code blue" was called, accompanied by a scramble of doctors and others with the red crash cart. As they crowded around Anna's bed working feverishly, Dwight and I sank to our knees in the hallway, praying only "Please, Jesus."

After a long time the medical crew said she was calling "Mom" under the oxygen mask and they made a space to let me approach her head. She looked up, then with a weak, awkward motion, grabbed my arm and with as much intensity as she could muster said a word neither I nor the nurses could understand. After repeating it several times, I realized she was saying "boys."

She was dying, and her greatest concern was for her brothers. How enormously she loved those two young men, her womb mates. I told her they were back at the house and encouraged her just to rest, and only then did she settle back and close her eyes.

From the journal:

I have come to the place where I can give Anna up to Jesus, if that is His plan. Still, in my heart I think of Abraham and Isaac and hope there is yet a ram in the thicket.

Patients in the ICU are not allowed overnight visitors, but after some consideration the Lord softened their hearts to allow me to sit in a chair beside Anna's bed. It has been a very long night, but I am deeply grateful for the privilege. Every time she opened her eyes, I have been here as promised. God has been faithful to help us keep that promise.

I have a speck of comprehension of His loving intent as our Heavenly Father, "I will never leave you nor forsake you."

He never has and never will.

Monday evening after surgery Dr. Dipersio came in to talk with us, confirming that Anna's condition was very grave and that we should make important decisions now about life support, etc.

From the journal:

He genuinely cares about Anna and it was hard for him to share such a grim report. His feeling is that her condition will continue to deteriorate until she "slips away." We thanked him and told him we would pray for wisdom. He left, and many tears followed.

From the journal:

Jim Fleshman called Dwight from England. He hammered in that we must not give up yet—not until and if God gives that final word. That was a real reinforcement.

Linda and her dad and others from the church were with us to cry and pray and encourage.

I'm grateful to have had that time to cry and have reiterated my former determination that every day Anna is alive we will focus on life and joy and, yes, even Heaven, as that blessed hope is certainly a part of life. If God's plan is to take Anna on to Heaven soon, I am resolved to make this, with His help, the very best possible passage for her from here to there. There is no room for self-pity. It is not fair to her; it robs us of time and energy that must be spent on her. The Lord will help us.

Every single day I have left with Anna is precious. I must not squander one of them wallowing in self-pity. Lord Jesus, please help me. I am weak, but You are strong.

This week-end Anna asked, "Mom, I just don't understand. Our family is so perfect, why does something have to mess it up?"

This was another of those harder-than-hard questions to which there are no answers. We were able to come to one conclusion: Sickness or even death can't "mess up" a family who love each other and love the Lord as much as ours does.

We are bound together by the promise that one day we will all be together in Heaven with Jesus. We are bound together by the greatest of human love cemented by Divine love. We are bound together by a wealth of happy memories and a thousand expressions of esteem, appreciation, and affirmation through the years, because we genuinely consider one another to be God's special gifts to each other. We are "tight," in the current vernacular use.

No, Anna, this doesn't "mess up" our family. Yes, it does change the game plan and certainly grieves us to consider a temporary separation, but our circle will be eternally bound together. Please rest assured in that.

Anna, her head all wrapped in white gauze and tape, is catheterized and both legs encased in devices to electronically stimulate circulation. There are tubes and lines and sensors everywhere. She opened her eyes a little while ago and stirred the covers with great effort to move. She uttered her first words–"Please–help."

I asked if she needed to go to the bathroom, and she nodded. I explained the catheter's presence and use, but in a few minutes she repeated, "Please." It tore my heart to look into those precious, beloved eyes born from my womb and feel so incapable to really help.

I wish this was a nightmare and morning would come. I look at her innocent, angelic face on the pillow, so sweet and trusting. Always the compliant child, Anna has consistently and conscientiously followed every direction and cooperated fully in each step of this agonizing journey. I look at her now and think of all the times she has willingly succumbed to things that hurt or tasted bad or were generally gross because we asked her to.

She has done everything we asked because she trusted us. I look at her now and feel like a traitor. I have betrayed her simple trust. She has done everything I ever asked of her without complaint or argument. Now she lies before me in pain, every part of her body affected by this hideous disease. The nurse has given her more medication. They have orders from Dr. Randy Brown and Dr. Dipersio that pain control is top priority.

Her cheeks are as rosy and pink as ever. In profile as I sit beside her, that tiny turned-up nose still intrigues and delights me. It is unlike Dwight's or mine—one of her special legacies from Sweet Granny, whose twinkling eyes and turned-up little nose have repeated themselves in her great-grandchild. A picture Aunt Rachel sent us recently of Granny and Anna when Anna was about two years old, both wearing matching flannel nightgowns, showed clear resemblance and also their love for one another. Anna's lips were naturally cherry-colored then, and they are just that shade tonight. I put clear lip gloss on them earlier because they're so dry, and they look as if they'd been painted.

She is truly a beautiful child, inside and out. I never knew a purer heart, a soul more sincere in seeking what is true and right. I love this child with my whole being, and only the Heavenly Father, who watched the death of His own Son, can comprehend the depth of my grief tonight.

Ironically, the surgical biopsy revealed that lesions in Anna's brain were caused by a fierce aspergillius fungal infection. There was no, NO evidence of cancer.

No leukemia. No malignancy. Anna was cancer free.

Dwight and I were stunned. How we had prayed for that news, and it had come to pass. How could this crazy infection in her brain threaten to take her out in spite of the victory over leukemia?

"Lord, are you hearing all of this? Helloooooo??? Are You hearing the throngs of pray-ers who are fasting and crying out to You today?"

TRIBULATION

By Friday the medical teams of each discipline had given up on Anna.

Dr. Dipersio and Dr. Brown told us they had never seen anyone survive an aspergillius infection in the brain. Dr. Dipersio ordered that Anna be transferred back up to the Bone Marrow Transplant unit, thirteenth floor, where she was known and loved. The staff there would care for her and us until she quietly slipped away. God sent Dr. Benjamin Tan, a rotating bone marrow transplant fellow who had been saved at a Billy Graham Crusade in the Philippines. Dr. Tan took one look at us and ordered, "Get a bed for the mother." It was placed right next to Anna.

The neurosurgery team led by Dr. Dacy concluded that any other procedures on their part would be uncalled for, as they would not alter the outcome. A young resident, Dr. Shahadi, who was expecting his own first son, was assigned the task of relaying the neurosurgery message to us. Someone in the hall when he left said the young doctor was weeping openly.

Our only hold-out was Dr. Vicky Frazier of Infectious Diseases. She had encouraged us to "go for it," that Anna really did have a small chance to get well. On Friday Dr. Frazier threw in the towel as well, telling us the only thing keeping Anna here was Mama's determined insistence. She gently offered the theological challenge that I was wrestling with God; He wanted her and I was still clinging to her. Anna would not leave until I would give her up. And I was not ready to do that.

From the journal:

Last night Dr. Dipersio came in. He looked at sleeping Anna with great tenderness and kindly asked Dwight and me if there was anything he could do for us.

I asked him to please not give up on her, to which he replied with a sad expression that he hasn't given up, but that medically they have done all they can do. He even went so far as to say, "You know, we are only the caregivers. We don't really do any healing."

We asked again if the leukemia is in remission. His reply was hesitant, then he just let it out: "Let's face it. Anna's leukemia is impossible. Her graft versus host is impossible. Now she has an infection that's impossible. Do you understand that?"

I nodded and quietly reminded him, "But she can still get well."

He gave us a wry smile, looked over at Dwight and said, "It would take a miracle."

We pressed him. "Do you concede, then, that if Anna gets well it would be a miracle?"

His quick, animated response: "If she gets well, I'll call in the archbishop and have this room canonized!"

Dwight led us in prayer before Dr. Dipersio left. Then we sat with Anna in silence for a very long time, contemplating the previous discussion, both of us pondering the will and course of God in the events of these days.

Contrary to popular belief on the floor, evidenced by many kind hugs and murmurs of sympathy, etc., I am not being "strong" or "holding up well." I just really do believe that God can heal Anna.

Hours stretched into days and days into weeks. Anna did not die.

She remained unconscious but breathed on her own. Fevers would come and go. The liver, heart, brain, lungs each took turns with problems and infections. But she did not die.

Our caring nurses tried to lovingly prepare me for the inevitable, especially when they came in during our daily "passive range of motion" exercises, in which I manually flexed Anna's legs to keep them in shape for running track, all while she lay unconscious. It must have been a sight.

Dwight came every day and spent several nights with us when conditions were perilous. Somehow he continued to juggle care for the boys, Grandmother, and the church, with time for us. What a prince. Through it all, he never missed a Sunday in the pulpit, and the Parkway congregation told us his preaching had never been more powerful. He felt led to fast and pray for forty days, juice only. He did this without fanfare; the only evidence his shrinking waistline.

Our Parkway church family maintained a twenty-four hour daily prayer vigil and manned a small waiting room down the hall on thirteenth floor, receiving telephone messages, most long distance, and always available to pray. They met and ministered to families of other patients on the floor as well, a living testimony of Christ's presence and care.

One day Josh came into Anna's room with a package of big red sourball candies and explained, "I found these in one of the machines and I know Anna really likes them." We put them on her bed-tray table so she could see them and have one as soon as she woke up from the coma. He turned to leave, then came back and with a felt tip pen scrawled "Josh" on the package label so she would know they were from him.

Josh also noticed on Saturday that Jonathan was fasting for their sister. Church members who took the boys out to eat at Union Station said Jonathan politely and unobtrusively declined to eat while sitting willingly with them at the table enjoying their delicious suppers. This was our growing fourteen-year-old son whom we accused of having hollow legs in which to pack so many hamburgers. I have never been more proud of him.

Late during that night/wee morning following Jonathan's fast day, nurse Dianne and I were changing Anna's gown and bed linens. As I bent to place things in the laundry sack, a dearly familiar voice spoke very clearly, "Mom."

Dianne asked, "Did you hear that?" and confirmed that I was not dreaming.

Anna was looking directly at me and had called my name. It was a priceless treasure. I cannot put into words the emotion that swept over my soul in that moment.

From the journal:

"It was the sweetest sound I know. I weep now as I write. Lord, please don't count it as unbelief. It's my heart overflowing."

S. . .l. . . o. . . w. . .l. . . y but surely, Anna began inching back to life. Dr. Jim Fleshman was first to notice a miniscule twitch of her toe under the sheet. He almost shouted with elation, "That's it! She's coming back!" Dwight and I agreed and held fast to hope.

Twitches became movements, sounds became words, and smiles showed us the light in her spirit still shining brightly.

What a happy treat the Lord gave us a little while ago. Anna was wide awake and I asked her to let me do some mouth care for her. She opened her mouth for me to insert the pink foam toothette and let me move it around, then released it without clenching her teeth. That was a first!

I reached for a second toothette: "That's great! Let's try it again."

This time she looked straight ahead and pursed her lips together in a firm lock.

I nudged them with the edge of the pink foam, but to no avail. I looked right into her eyes and said, "Anna, if you don't open your mouth, I'm going to spank you."

To my amazement, she not only smiled, but actually laughed! I was so surprised, I thought maybe it was just imagined.

"Anna, are you laughing?" I peered down at her. "Do you think I won't spank you just because you're sick?" Again, she laughed and smiled. When we retold it later to nurse Melissa, she smiled again!

"Anna's bodyguards," we called the big, highly skilled orderlies who came to lift her into a chair and then back into bed. Two of them would each carefully hold two corners of her white bed sheet and then, in perfect synchrony on count of three, lift her in that white hammock to swing gently into the nearby upholstered chair, returning later to reverse the process.

They, like many others, took personal ownership in their care for Anna. Nurse Therese told us the nurses were surprised by the number of calls received at the desk from other departments in the hospital asking about Anna.

Little by little, Anna was coming back to the amazement of everyone. We celebrated every tiny success, like this journal entry:

From the journal:

Good news to report! Last night Anna freely moved her head at will and used her right hand to scratch her nose. This morning when Jane was working with her catheter, she voluntarily moved her right leg. The Lord is good. An MRI has been scheduled for today to see how much the lesions have decreased.

The next day's journal entry reads:

In talking to Gloria (BMT unit pharmacist) today, she said everyone on staff is utterly baffled by Anna's case. In every recorded instance of aspergillius infection in the brain, patients never awakened from comas.

In Anna's case, as we learned yesterday from her doctors, the MRI shows the legions to be larger, more dense, and more in number than on the previous MRI of her brain. That being the case, it is an incongruous paradox that clinically she is improving each day.

Last night, after we had received the devastating medical report and dealt with her doctors about an unauthorized DNR issue, Anna asked verbally for ice, chewed and swallowed it, and asked her Dad what time it was. This morning she shocked Dr. Frazier by telling her she does not like to be suctioned (used to get the junk from her mouth and throat).

Oddly, instead of feeling pulled as in a medical tug-of-war, I still feel the greatest peace and real hope in our Lord of Lords who created Anna and gave her to us and the world fourteen years ago despite medical odds. He alone rules and reigns, and He alone will decide Anna's future.

It seems like we are up on Mt. Carmel (13th floor) and the prophets of Baal and the prophets of God are waiting to see whose stack of wood will be struck by fire. Our wood is definitely wet, and for it to be ignited would be a clear clarion call to recognize the glory and majesty of the only Great Creator and Healer and Lord of all. He appeared as a flame in the burning bush before Moses and then led the children of Israel though the wilderness as a pillar of fire. He appeared on the Day of Pentecost in the form of "tongues of fire" resting on each of the believers gathered in the upper room in Jerusalem.

Oh, Lord, send your fire down to Anna's hospital room in power and deliverance. Reveal Yourself to all who look on. Let her be a living testimony to the reality of the one true God, who is the same yesterday, today, and tomorrow. Let each of us tremble in conviction, repentance, and surrender to the Lord of Lords who bore all our sin and infirmities on the cross and then arose victorious from the grave.

Two nights ago Bonita was our nurse. As she finished helping us change bed linens during the night, I thanked her for her kindness. Her reply was,

"Mrs. Blankenship, I love Anna."

"Thank you, Bonita."

She added, "Mrs. Blankenship, every nurse up here loves Anna."

I smiled, deeply touched.

Bonita went on, "We love you and the Reverend, too."

Thanking her, I asked if she had ever had an opportunity to know Jesus in a personal way.

Her reply was the song of a meadowlark to my heart: "Oh, yes ma'am. I'm saved. I'm a member of *Mt. Carmel* Baptist Church, and my church has been praying for Anna."

Sunday, December 3, the journal entry again includes reference to Elijah on Mt. Carmel.

From the journal:

Our wood is very, very wet. A few nights ago Dr. Dipersio reiterated to us the hopelessness of Anna's situation, using the term "impossible" three times in a row—impossible leukemia (their records now call it CML with Philadelphia chromosome and Monosomy 7); impossible graft versus host disease, unrelenting after four months of treatment; and impossible infection, fungal aspergillius in the central nervous system.

Three times water was poured upon Elijah's altar of faith, and three times water has been poured upon the altar of our faith, threatening to douse all hope from our hearts.

Yet here we are again today, the joy of the Lord still our strength, His faithfulness our only hope. It is the best place to be.

With the excellent help of speech therapist Ellen, Anna's sounds became words. This straight A student was now learning ABC's, how to count, days of the week, colors, and how to tell time. She could name opposites and tell stories about herself and our family. Curiously, she could more easily sing words than speak them, chiming in with Christmas carols played in our room.

The Philippians 4 passage we had memorized now came back easily. She might not be able to say "cat" or "dog," but at the word "rejoice," she would take it and run. "Rejoice in the Lord always, and again I say, rejoice. Let your forbearing spirit be known to all men; the Lord is near. Be anxious for nothing, but in everything by prayer and supplication, let your request be made known to God...."

And she would continue to quote the entire passage. It was amazing.

She blessed us all by quoting Scriptures with me. Dwight cried.

Jim Fleshman takes fresh glazed doughnuts for Joshua and Jonathan's Sunday School class every Sunday. He joined us in Anna's room and asked what she wants him to bring her.

"Dough. . . dough. . . dough-rings!"

Such determination! Anna's diligence at every turn was apparent. Her dream remained to walk and then run again. The nurses had her track shoes sterilized and hung them from a ceiling IV hook along with a bright red quilted stocking from Mary Engelbreit imprinted, "Believe."

Simple hand gestures, movement of a toe, a swallow of strawberry ice cream, and her steadily progressing verbal skills brought elation to her cheering section and spurred Anna to work even harder.

We played guessing games to communicate what she clearly intended to say.

For example, one night we had brushed teeth and said prayers and lain down. I was almost asleep when she started trying to say something. As we lay in the semi-darkness, I tried to translate what she was saying but couldn't understand. Standing over her, we tried again.

"Something hurt?"

"No."

"Something you need?"

"No."

"Someone?"

"Yes."

"Joyce?"

"No."

"Sounds like 'Joyce'?"

"Yes."

"Someone from Texas?"

"No."

"Someone in our family?"

"No."

"Someone from Daddy's church?"

"Yes."

"Hmmm. . . someone from the church, sounds like Joyce–BOYS. . . the boys' friend, Mr. Brasfield?"

"Yes!"

"We need to pray for Mr. Brasfield?"

A vigorous head shaking and verbal "Yes."

Back on my knees beside her bed, we prayed again, this time for Mr. Brasfield, whose name I had forgotten to lift to the Lord in our earlier prayer. But Anna had not forgotten and would not rest until we prayed for him.

Anna took very seriously her commitment to pray for individuals. Mary called one afternoon to let Anna know she was on her way to New York as a morning guest on the "Today" show. I was excited that we would get to see Mary on TV, but Anna's heart was in praying for her safe plane flight.

She prayed for other patients on the bone marrow unit, and sometimes asked me to step down to their rooms to check on them for her or to pass along candy or other treats.

There were often great needs other than medical ones, both for patients and staff.

Anna cared about each one and faithfully prayed.

Many patients on the unit did not survive. When someone died, it reminded us painfully of the fragility of life in general and especially on our floor.

One of those special patient friends was a lady named Cathy. When she was able, a nurse would roll her into Anna's room for Sunday church. Cathy, who had recently lost her eyesight, was fascinated by the Bible reading and thoroughly enjoyed our creaky singing.

Anna began praying that God would restore Cathy's sight. She sent me down to Cathy's room with peach tea, her favorite, and some colored translucent "stick-ons" for her window to brighten up the room even though Cathy herself could not see. The journal records, "We traced outlines on the cool glass of the window with Cathy's fingers as I described the colors of pretty flowers. She seemed to have a childlike fascination for the peelable pictures."

After one Sunday service, Cathy sent word asking me to come to her room and repeat the words of a hymn so her sister could write them down for her. We talked more about Jesus and the peace He could give.

Three days later, Anna and I were awakened early in the morning by Cathy's sister, who had come to tell us that she had just passed away. It was hard news to hear. Anna cried for her friend and remembered that she had been praying for Cathy's sight. We wrote in the journal, "Today she must have beheld all the glories of Heaven and Jesus Himself with perfect vision."

All of Anna's nurses were incredible. No adjectives are adequate to describe their dedicated skill and compassion. Donna Gallagher, one of the best, was her nurse on the day Cathy died. This was recorded in the journal:

The nurses have been somewhat somber as they went about their duties on the floor. Precious Donna was Anna's nurse today. We had a long talk about life and death, then when I was in the shower she and Donna talked about it and even prayed together.

These nurses are wonderful. They lose so many patients on this floor, yet they still allow their hearts to remain tender and vulnerable. The fact that they do care so deeply certainly costs them in terms of emotional expenditure, yet they are finer nurses for it. Their skills are honed to excellence by the drive to give their best to the patients they serve.

Other patients came and went, and some returned repeatedly. We were encouraged by those who returned to visit looking healthy and fit, like Mrs. Hix.

Her exuberant recovery helped Anna realize some people really did come out of transplants well and whole. Through it all, Anna just kept at it.

From the journal:

Yesterday when Ellen (speech therapist) was here, Anna worked hard and did well but became frustrated that it is still not perfect. When we affirmed her good work, she said, "No, it was terrible."

Ellen laughed and countered, "Anna! A week ago you couldn't even say 'terrible'!"

The journal also records our surprise and that of nurse Elise when Anna asked, "Is Elise going to bring my Vancomycin?" That would be a mouthful for anyone, but especially for a little girl whose third MRI showed still more new lesions in her brain, even as she was making dramatic progress. Go figure.

Anna dreaded MRI's. Her resistance to that closed tube never got better, even though the technicians allowed me to sit in a chair next to her head with my arm and hand inside the machine holding hers. For the last two MRI's, Dr. Hanna Khoury promised Anna Belgian chocolates mailed to the U.S. from his brother-in-law in Europe just for her. Really? Really. Both times she cooperated, and both times he gallantly delivered.

Dr. Powderly, Anna's new Irish infectious disease doctor, reaffirmed the priority of clinical assessment over test results, and he also reaffirmed that she was definitely better. He said her progress was a mystery to him and to all the other doctors. He, nor any of his colleagues, had ever seen or known of anyone to "come around" from an aspergillius fungal infection coma as Anna had. This was new ground where no one had ever walked before.

It felt sort of like "walking on the water" with Jesus, and we were definitely holding on to Him for the ride. Anna began taking oral doses of a new drug Dr. Arribas read about in a medical journal from Spain. Still another infectious disease specialist, Dr. Johnson, came in to meet Anna. He looked, asked questions, then smiled, "Anna, you may not realize it, but you are a legend in the infectious disease world."

BMT Dr. Randy Brown, Dr. Dipersio's associate, even used the "m" word–"miracle."

BLESSINGS

Christmas was coming. Barb Watson brought some shiny green tinsel that we taped to the window in the shape of a tree with gold tinsel above it bent into a star. It was beautiful, especially at night when bright lights from cars in the busy traffic far below made moving patterns of lights on our tree! Christmas had always been special for our family, and this would be no exception.

When the children were small I had sewed them a soft fabric nativity crèche from cotton prints with Mary and Joseph, baby Jesus, shepherds, wise men, and angels. To keep the arms from sticking straight out, each doll's hands were stitched together in front.

Anna especially enjoyed playing with the soft doll figures, moving them around and speaking parts for them. One day I overheard her cherub voice as Mary, "That's O.K. You can hold my baby."

When I peeked in, baby Jesus had been tucked into the arms of one of the bearded shepherd dolls where he remained. Anna's role play conveyed a strong message about the first Christmas in Bethlehem.

When God's Son came to earth in human flesh as a baby, his mother prepared for the birth by packing clean white cloths for "swaddling" him. The Bible says the night he was born in a Bethlehem stable (no room in the inn), she wrapped him in swaddling clothes and laid him in the manger, which Joseph surely filled with fresh hay before laying the newborn baby on the makeshift mattress.

If Mary was like most new moms, she did her best to keep her little one clean and safe. Today's number one rule when approaching a newborn: "Wash your hands!"

How unusual, then, that the first visitors, not only invited but commanded by the heavenly host of angels, were shepherds who lived outside in the fields with their sheep.

Bedouin shepherds were rough nomads, sleeping on the ground in the most crude conditions. Washing? Bathing? Unknown to these fellows.

But it was these unlikely visitors, probably accompanied by their flock of animals, who first appeared at the stable to see the new baby. When Mary, after her long donkey ride through the mountains, labor and delivery in a stable, and now post partum, saw the untidy strangers peering in, what was her response?

Scripture is silent at this point, but my imagination can picture little Anna's kind words for Mary, "You can hold my baby." And pure, innocent God-Child, Jesus, Emanuel "God with us," was lovingly placed in the gnarled trembling hands of a shepherd.

The Bible says Mary "pondered those things and kept them in her heart."

Me, too.

Jesus came to shepherds, and He also came to us. That night it was a stable in Bethlehem. This Christmas, it was a hospital room in Queeny Tower overlooking St. Louis. I whispered with the hymn writer, "Come into my heart, Lord Jesus. There is room in my heart for Thee."

Christmas Day Dwight brought Josh, Jonathan, and Grandmother about noon to open packages we had been stacking on the windowsill under our "tree." He read the Christmas story from Luke 2 and Jonathan read Santa's annual letter left taped to the "tree." Midway through, he looked up and commented, "This is sounding less and less like Santa."

Every Christmas Mrs. Santa made Anna a new Sunday dress and a matching one for her Christmas doll. I had once asked Anna how long she thought she might like to keep getting dolls for Christmas. She paused to consider it, then replied, "I think until I'm fourteen." This year it was a china doll dressed in white, the color of Anna's bed sheets. She was fourteen years old.

By the way, many families struggle with the issue of Santa. At our house, the children came home from kindergarten one day reporting that one of their playmates had declared Santa "not real." Uh-oh. The inevitable dilemma. We chose to face it honestly. I answered the children's sincere question truthfully, explaining that Santa was pretend, but Jesus was real.

That question settled, I went on to offer that as long as we would "pretend" about Santa, we would have presents. To this day, we celebrate the real Christ of Christmas and the pretend fun of Santa—with presents.

January 7, Anna and I decided to observe Epiphany, commemorating the wise men's arrival in Bethlehem. It inspired us to remember how God led them away from all that was familiar to venture into the unknown, their focus on His star alone. The long journey must have been arduous, but their resolve was strong. They were on their way to see Jesus! With every camel clop, the cherished goal drew closer.

Gifts from the magi were lavish expressions of their heartfelt adoration. In God's divine plan, Joseph probably used frankincense, gold, and myrrh to provide for the young family's needs when they fled to safety in Egypt from the jealous wrath of King Herod. Long before the words of Romans 8:28 were penned by Apostle Paul, that principle was demonstrated in events surrounding the birth of Jesus.

To celebrate Epiphany, Saturday night we asked the nurses to fetch slippers of their patients and to set them in the hall outside their doors. In our room Anna watched from her bed as I prepared tissue pouches of individually wrapped candies and tied them with brightly colored ribbon bows. Notes were written to each patient about the wise men's journey and the sense of promise their experience inspired in us for the transplant process.

What a peculiar, happy sight—the entire hallway of 13th floor lined with all varieties of adult footwear, out of which poufed tissue paper, ribbons and goodwill!

All through Anna's amazing comeback, her progress was often interrupted by medical setbacks—infections, pneumonia, severe pain, persistent nausea, and many other issues. One morning she woke me before daylight saying her bed was shaking. When I scrambled up to look, *she* was shaking and jerking, reminiscent of the earlier two seizures. It lasted about two minutes. Her nurse and doctor on duty rushed in. Anna remained fully conscious. Two more episodes by 8:30 AM were troubling but were deemed not to be seizures, probably involuntary muscle spasms.

The journal records notes of fear and prayers, seeking the Lord's help in times of great distress.

I have a bit of a sick feeling in the pit of my stomach, a twinge of dread. Lord, you have never wavered once in Your faithfulness to us. "Neither death, nor life, nor angels, nor principalities, nor things present, not things to come, nor powers, nor height, nor depth, nor any other created thing shall be able to separate us from the love of God, which is in Christ Jesus our Lord." Romans 8:38–39.

A verse across on the left side of the page catches my eye because it has been underlined and "starred"–"For I consider that the sufferings of this present time are not worthy to be compared with the glory that is to be revealed to us."

Anna belongs to the Lord. He knows the love for her in my heart, and that is magnified a trillion zillion times in His love for her. He knows my agony because He made me, too, and knows every part of me inside and out.

Thank You for Your steadfast kindness that never lets us go. Father, please hold us in the palm of Your great hand and carry us gently through these days. You created this, my beloved child, flesh of my flesh, and knit her into my heart. I entrust her to You, Whose grace is sufficient.

There was a lot of prayer going up in many different ways. In emergencies it was the S.O.S. "Help!"

Evening prayers kneeling beside Anna's bed were our daily ritual. Early morning quiet times with Bible and journal were often interrupted by doctors' visits, tests, and therapies.

Dwight entered a forty day fast.

Our Parkway family prayed around the clock. One dear brother, Greg Cunningham, retreated in seclusion to fast and pray for days.

Nurses told us they and their family members lit prayer candles for Anna. Many said their churches were praying at their request.

Our gifted BMT chaplain, Julie Allen Berger, would often ask, "Would a prayer be helpful?" We would bow heads together as she prayed simply and sincerely for Anna and our family.

Churches all over America and around the world heard about Anna in various ways and sent word of their fervent prayers.

Dr. Khoury said his parents in Lebanon, Orthodox Christians, were praying for Anna. On more than one Saturday, his personal time off, Hanna returned to the hospital bringing his wife Angela and two small children. He would stay with their little ones at the nurses' station while Angela knelt beside Anna's bed in earnest silent prayer.

Reflection on these prompted memory and recording of a story in the journal.

From the journal:

I am reminded of a lesson the Lord taught me two years ago when the children were in sixth grade at Bailey, their first year in middle school. Dr. Roy Fish was preaching a revival at the church, and during the invitation hymn I knelt at my pew to pray about a very persistent and difficult problem. While kneeling there, the idea came that I should fast until the problem was solved. What?! I could starve to death!

The night I promised the Lord to begin the fast, it was with no idea what fasting involved or how it worked, only that I would try it with His help. The next morning as the children were leaving for school, Josh asked for an extra twenty-five cents with his lunch. When I asked why, he explained that phone calls cost a quarter and maybe he should have one on hand just in case he would ever need to call home. That sounded reasonable, so the quarter dropped in with the rest, and off to school they went.

About ten o'clock the phone rang, and housework paused as I answered, "Hello?"

"Hi, Mom."

"Hi, Josh. What's up?"

"Oh, not much."

"Is everything O.K.?"

"Yes ma'am, everything's fine. Well, I guess I'd better be going."

"Alright. I love you."

"I love you, too. Bye, Mom."

"Good-bye, Josh."

I hung up the receiver and smiled. What a strange, funny call. But, then, life with Josh has never been dull and certainly not predictable. As I turned to resume daily tasks at hand, I stopped in my tracks. Of course!

Josh's call, with no apparent purpose, had seemed pointless. Now it was clear.

The middle school telephone was a pay phone. Josh had never used a pay phone before. This new gizmo hanging in the school hallway piqued Josh's interest in a brand new way to "call home."

God used that incident with Josh to teach me about prayer with fasting. There was no set of "do's" and "don'ts." God knew my heart's desire was just to "call home" and here was another way to do it.

By February Anna was able in physical therapy to stand alone and then to take steps with parallel bars, a monumental step toward her goal of walking again. She was also yellow as a pumpkin as her bilirubin count climbed. Even her eyes were yellow.

Fevers and weakness followed; her liver was in serious trouble, and terrible pain indicated the likelihood of pancreatitis. On days when she was too weak to talk much, she remained fully alert. We often turned to Psalms.

From the journal:

Psalm 73:26, "My flesh and my heart may fail; but God is the strength of my heart and my portion forever."

When Uncle W.C. died suddenly in 1983, Sweet Granny grieved so deeply for him, all of us were very concerned for her. She did not grieve "as those who have no hope," because she knew he was in Heaven and that one day she would see him again, but her mother heart was clearly broken.

Aunt Rachel told us that once when she and Granny were visiting the family cemetery next to Evergreen Church, she tried to comfort Granny by reminding her of the assurance of Heaven, "the blessed hope" she had taught them when they were children. Sweet Granny, her short frame bent over, her white hair bun glistening in the sun, thrust her walking cane down into the fresh dirt covering the grave.

"Yes, I know what the Bible says, and I know that W.C. is in Heaven with Jesus; but the part of him that I gave birth to and held and touched is right there, and that's the part I grieve for."

In Texas with three small children, I could not be with Granny in her grief, although we talked on the telephone every morning at 7:45. Psalm 73:26 became the special verse I prayed for her many times over the years.

In the last week or so Anna has grown increasingly weak and her bilirubin has soared. She is fully conscious but too weak to talk very much. Her temperature is 38.8 Centigrade this morning and no cultures are growing from the blood draws to help identify a source of infection. Her condition is grave. In our morning devotionals we have been reading Psalms; somehow I always turn there when things are hard.

Psalm 73 talks about David's inner conflict when he had trusted God and sought to keep his heart pure, yet found himself in great adversity. On the other hand, he observed those who were blatantly wicked apparently prospering even as they blasphemed the righteous God.

David's sense of injustice threatened to rock his faith, but by the end of the Psalm he could serenely affirm again, "My flesh and my heart may fail; but God is the strength of my heart and my portion forever." I have read it several times recently.

Friday Anna asked, "Why did God let this happen to me?"

There was anguish in her voice and on her face as she looked into mine, and there I stood stricken dumb, utterly stumped to comprehend WHY. Why sweet Anna??? The very foundation of our confession is the bedrock conviction that (1) He *is,* and (2) that He is *able.* So why doesn't He heal her? Today? Right now?

I have not one answer except that He hears us and that He loves us.

The Bible says, "Faith is the evidence of things not seen," and that is certainly where I am now–groping through the murky darkness, yet always cognizant of a rope tied securely around me and around Anna that will not let us go. I have to believe that somehow, somewhere there is light at the end of this hideous tunnel and it is Jesus Himself, the Light of the World, our Good Shepherd.

As if on cue (Divine appointment? I think so), Saturday Dwight brought in a mail parcel from Texas, a framed cross stitched sampler from Dianne McFadden to thank me for staying with her parents the Welches at the hospital when her dad was sick. The simple sampler reads, "My flesh and my heart may fail; but God is the strength of my heart and my portion forever."

Yes, You are here. Please hold us gently and carry us through today.

During Anna's long hospitalization we bought a newspaper every Saturday for the weekly television schedule which was quickly scanned and noted for ice skating programs. She loved them.

She knew all the skaters by name, but her all time favorite was Paul Wylie. Several years earlier in Texas she had heard an interview with Paul in which he said his greatest ambition in life was not to win the Olympic gold medal but to glorify Jesus Christ. From that time on, Anna committed in her heart to pray for Paul Wylie that God would protect him from injury and bless his performances. Every time we watched a skating event, she would look for Paul Wylie and pray for him.

In February, at the height of Anna's terrible liver and pancreas setback, we heard that Paul Wylie and a bunch of other professional skaters would be in St. Louis for a big exhibition performance. I wrote a note to him, which Dwight delivered to the Ritz Carlton Hotel. Late Friday afternoon before the evening performance, the phone rang. Paul Wylie for Anna! She was thrilled.

Saturday he sent to the hospital by courier an autographed souvenir program for Anna. Under his picture in bold black marker, Paul Wylie had signed his name and the Scripture reference "Philippians 4:4–7," the very passage we had memorized back in the summer. Anna could even now rattle off the familiar passage: "Rejoice in the Lord always. . . ." What a great encouragement! It was also a handy tool as the journal records.

From the journal:

How appropriate that passage has been in these recent days as we faced new obstacles with liver problems, etc. Also, several of the doctors at various points in the last week or so have queried Anna with such questions as "Where are you?" "What year is this?" "What is your address?" Some told us, in her presence, that she is apparently "mentally impaired" because she did not know her address (we don't have one) or missed the correct year (Mom loses track of that, too, especially since we sort of slid into this one).

Now when that comes up, we just inquire, "Did you hear who called Anna?"

Anna tells about Paul Wylie's call. Then we ask, "Would you like to see what he sent over?"

Of course they are obligated to look at the autographed picture.

"And you see right here (pointing) there's a reference. Do you know what it is? "

To date, none of them have been able to respond.

"Anna, why don't you help him."

Anna deftly begins quoting the long passage word for word.

No more questions.

Anna's hospital chaplain, Julie Berger, offered us spiritual care and dear support. One day she asked me at what point we would be willing to say "enough" and stop medical treatment. My instant reply was "never." Anna was only fourteen. If and when she went to Heaven, it would be because the Lord in

His wisdom took her. I could only accept that if we had done everything we could for her here. I still believed Anna could get well. That is not every family's position, but it was ours.

Julie told me she had heard a man from Harvard speak at a seminar who talked about the terrible plight of our world—bad things all around us—but said, nevertheless, he was a "prisoner of hope." She said she thought of us and found that label appropriate for my own spirit, a "prisoner of hope."

From the journal:

Job said, "Though He slay me, yet will I trust in Him." My NASB translation reads, "Though He slay me, I will hope in Him. Nevertheless, I will argue my ways before Him." Job 13:15.

A beloved hymn reads, "My hope is built on nothing less than Jesus' blood and righteousness. I dare not trust the sweetest frame but wholly lean on Jesus' name."

Estelle Hymans, my Jewish friend and Ellen's mom, sent us a wonderful poem in today's mail.

"Keep Swimming"

Two frogs fell into a deep cream bowl.

One was an optimistic soul.

But the other took the gloomy view.

"We'll drown," he lamented without more ado,

and with a last despairing cry

he flung up his legs and said "Good-bye."

Quote the other frog with a steadfast grin,

"I can't get out, but I won't give in.

I'll just swim around till my strength is spent,

then I'll die the more content."

Bravely he swam to work his scheme,

and his struggles began to churn the cream.

The more he swam, his legs a-flutter,

the more the cream turned into butter.

On top of the butter as last he stopped

and out of the bowl he gaily hopped.

What is the moral? It's easily found. . .

If you can't hop out, keep swimming around!

FEBRUARY 12:

"Before I formed you in the womb, I knew you in the womb. I knew you, and before you were born I consecrated you... Do not be afraid of them, for I am with you to deliver you, declares the Lord... I am watching over My word to perform it... they will fight against you, but they will not overcome you, for I am with you to deliver you, declares the Lord," Jeremiah 1:5,8,12,19.

In this opening chapter of Jeremiah, God bolsters Jeremiah's spirit with words of promise. God knew even before Jeremiah was born that he would face testing and hardship, but in every oppression God would be with him to see him safely through.

Lord, are these verses for us, too?

Anna threw up all last night and all morning today. It is very dark like coffee. Her fever is down, for which we are grateful, but she is as weak as a little rag doll. I hold her close and she rests her head against me, even when she is vomiting into the pink barf basin. I love her dearly. Only the Lord Himself knows how much. He is our comfort.

11:30 PM Sitting in a chair beside Anna's bed. We've been bathing her arms and legs with tepid water to help bring her fever down from 40.4 C., 104.7 F. The abdominal x-ray this afternoon showed pancreatitis. Pain medicine is in the IV every three hours around the clock without asking, even if she's asleep. Dr. Khoury has ordered nothing by mouth for at least two days, longer if necessary, not even water or ice chips. Nothing. No tube feeding either. She will receive fluids by IV, no TPN. It is another hard bump in her road.

We have been reading one of Grace Livingston Hill's circa 1900 novels, *Matched Pearls,* a recent gift to Anna. It's about a young woman's journey to becoming a Christian. The "handsome prince" in the story is named Seagrave, an odd name to us. Tonight I was reading the book aloud to Anna and was sort of surprised that this beautiful romantic story explains the need of the human soul to be changed to a clean new heart in Christ Jesus. The author quotes the Bible as part of the narrative.

When Anna's nurse Kelli came in, I was stricken with shyness for her to hear the bold assertions that everyone needs to be saved, no matter how "good" they might be.

I hesitated in the reading, but then timidly continued.

In a few minutes Kelli asked, "Say, the guy Seagrave. Is he a nice person?"

So, she was listening while busily working with Anna's IV medications. I told her that he was the hero of the story.

"Good," she went on; "Seagrave was my maiden name."

Coincidence? Kelli heard about the love of Jesus despite my reluctance, and the Lord even used her own name.

Kelli just now took Anna's temperature again. Still coming down. Thank you, Jesus. Chantey came in and helped me bathe her again. We prayed and sang hymns as we wiped her arms and legs. A few tears slipped down my cheeks, but Anna's eyes were closed.

The next day, February 13, Anna, sick as she was, took delight in our plan to surprise other patients on the unit with hand-made Valentines. Red heart-shaped doilies were centered with a pink paper heart inscribed "Happy Valentine's Day, John 13:34–35, Love, Anna." She was so happy for me to tiptoe down the hallway after most people were asleep, taping Valentines to each door to be discovered the following morning, February 14.

By February 19 she wanted me to read aloud from her American History textbook for "school," even with intense tummy pain and a billirubin up twelve points to 33. I journaled,

The Lord's angels must be encamped around our room. Her pain pierces my heart. How God could bear the suffering of His beloved Son Jesus on the cross is beyond my comprehension. I pray with every breath.

Over the following weeks Anna's bilirubin gradually decreased and so did her jaundice. Sometimes she became discouraged when progress seemed at a standstill, but her diligence to work hard at therapy and her positive spirit always prevailed. She dearly loved her nurses and they seemed to reciprocate, caring for her tenderly and repeatedly going the extra mile. Nurse Jane, who had administered the transplant, prayed giving her heart to Christ. So did Jennie and Peggy and others we heard from later.

From the journal:

It has been a week of great joy and great sorrow. Anna's special encourager, Mr. Earl Brasfield, was released from the agony of bone cancer to go home to Heaven. Dwight preached his funeral. Last night we listened to a tape of the service and were reminded again of the very temporary nature of this life and the eternal reality of Heaven.

(Later)

As I was writing the above paragraph, there was a knock on the door and to our surprise there stood the beautiful Mrs. Margaret Brasfield and her daughter Amy.

Mrs. Margaret smiled with a genuine radiance that could only come from the glow of Jesus deep within. Her poise is more than the cultured elegance of the world. She has the "peace that passes understanding."

From our hospital window there is a far-reaching view of Forest Park, site of the 1904 World's Fair—sloping green lawns with patches of majestic trees intertwined with well-used walking and biking trails. The fair was an exhibition whose grandeur was unprecedented in world civilization.

Dwight discovered a collection of pictures from that historic event in archives at the library when we were gathering material for the children's school research papers last Spring. We were awed by the incredibly lavish details on colossal structures, elaborate statues, and every kind of ornate flourish so popular in the golden Victorian era. Exhibits represented the best from each parent country, and the magnificent buildings were often reflected in pools of water, small lakes strategically designed to complement a spectacular landscape.

As we studied those aged illustrations, turning huge pages now yellowed in antiquity, Dwight and I both asked, almost in unison, "What happened to them?" "Where did they go?"

Pursuing the questions further with local citizens, we learned that the grand, opulent structures built for the 1904 World's Fair were constructed of chicken wire and plaster of Paris, fabulous to behold but temporary by design. They were intended to last one year and then weather and other elements would and did take their natural toll.

One local township tried to preserve a particular statue as a commemorative marker. They moved it to a prominent spot and coated the outside with some sort of protective solution and paint, but all their efforts were in vain. To their disappointment, the statue gradually broke and crumbled.

Today Forest Park's expanses of green grass and tall trees are dotted with small lakes and winding roadways, faint echoes from by-gone days of the great world exhibition.

Mr. Brasfield, Anna, and I were all created with temporary housing to accommodate our brief earthly stays. The spirit inside each of us is eternal; and when our appointed time here is finished, the spirit leaves the deteriorating body behind.

II Corinthians 5:1,6–9, "For we know that if the earthly tent which is our house is torn down, we have a building from God, a house not made with hands, eternal in the heavens. Therefore, being always of good courage, and knowing that while we are at home in the body we are absent from the Lord, for we walk by faith and not by sight—we are of good courage, I say, and prefer rather to be absent from the body and to be at home with the Lord. Therefore also we have as our ambition, whether at home or absent, to be pleasing to Him."

Anna's motivation to walk again was absolute. March 19 she graduated from parallel bars to the walker in physical therapy, a spectacular effort. Occupational therapist Carol Ponceroli helped her make brownies, which she shared with her nurses and sent some by Dad to Josh and Jonathan. It was a red-letter day!

All through Anna's hospitalization we were blessed by loved ones who traveled great distances to only stop in briefly and then return home again. They understood Anna's required quiet and isolation but wanted her and us to know that they cared.

We certainly did.

Anna was so happy that Uncle Floyd was driving "the Aunts," her great aunts, to St. Louis, she told every nurse and medical helper who came near her bed. When they got to St. Louis, found the hotel, showered and changed, and finally arrived at Barnes Hospital, it had been one long day. Imagine their surprise while waiting for the elevator on the ground floor of Queeny Tower (seventeen floors) when a total stranger looked at them and asked, "Are you the Aunts?"

"Church" in our hospital room every Sunday morning included whoever could slip in, and it was always special. We would sing and read the Bible and pray, knowing all too well that our little group was never the same. As Easter Sunday approached, Anna's goal became Sunday worship at Parkway. It was a worthy goal, but Dr. Dipersio made no promises.

Mrs. Tierney's (patient across the hall) daughter provided a huge stack of paper cutout rabbits in different colors. One night while Anna slept, I taped those rabbits in a continuous waving line all the way from the elevator, down the hall, around and back on the other side of the hallway, over the nurses' station, and back to the elevator. Rabbits everywhere! Next morning nurses and patients twittered about the booming rabbit population on 13th floor. When Anna's orderlies lifted her into the wheelchair and out the door, she gasped and giggled with delight. It was worth everything to see her smile.

Easter, April 8, Dr. Dipersio gave the O.K. and Anna's angel nurses carefully arranged her IV med schedules so that she could attend morning worship at Parkway.

A van equipped with a special wheelchair lift came to Barnes for us; and nurse Therese, on her personal day off, drove from Illinois to make the outing possible. All the nurses gathered around like mother hens preparing Anna for her first peek out of the hospital in five months. She wore a new yellow dress and the straw hat Sharon had sent adorned with silk sunflowers and geraniums.

Josh and Jonathan met us at the church door, proud and happy as could be, as Anna in the wheelchair was carefully unloaded and brought in to the back of the sanctuary where the service had already begun. Her brothers sat on the pew next to her wheelchair, and Dad beamed from the pulpit. Christ's resurrection granted new life, and we rejoiced in His promise together as a family.

Hooray!

Because of Anna's remarkable improvement, Dr. Dipersio announced, "This is becoming more like summer camp than the bone marrow transplant unit!" With that, he ordered a transfer over the walkway back to St. Louis Children's Hospital for more specific therapy and rehabilitation. Such a great progress report caused mixed feelings for melancholy Anna to leave her friends at Barnes.

Her speech, occupational, and physical therapists celebrated with a festive picnic on Monday, April 22, and the next day her nurses held a beautiful luncheon with balloons, crepe paper streamers from the ceiling, cake, sandwiches, and, of course, chips and salsa. They gave her new workout clothes, fragrant bath goodies, and a porcelain music box of children themed "You have touched many hearts." With tears, hugs, and helping hands from Parkway ladies, Anna moved back to Children's Hospital.

As predicted, with excellent therapy at Children's Hospital Anna continued to improve. She also blossomed in relationships previously forged with doctors, nurses, and patients there. Shelly and Debra, two of her favorites, planned a "slumber party" in her room on their personal off duty time, the ultimate demonstration of kindness. These two incredible nurses arrived in casual "civilian" clothes with movies and pizza, brownies, nachos, and every other goodie they thought she would like. Pillows and blankets piled in, too. Anna's delight made all of us happy.

Their gift not only blessed Anna but granted a "date night" for Dwight and me as well. Dinner, the St. Louis Symphony, and overnight in a nearby hotel seemed like a dream. We left Dwight's cell phone number with Anna, and she called every hour or two just to check in with us and to excitedly report about her own great adventure. On the Lord's list of "good works," one humongous addition was added for Shelly and Debra.

It was my only night away from Anna in fifteen months, but she was not alone.

Anna's walker switched to quad cane and quad cane to stick cane. Counting became math and then algebra. The feeding tube was used only at night for briefer periods until it was finally surgically removed. Tuesday, June 4, we received orders via Shelly to discontinue the last two IV medications for oral meds.

From the journal:

She began taking them orally tonight, and if the Lord blesses them to absorb correctly, she will be officially "free" of lines and poles for the first time in 368 days. YES!! *Thank You.*

Now that Anna was cancer-free, Dr. Michael Noetzel, pediatric neurologist, became her primary physician at Children's Hospital. Dr. Noetzel and his team plotted a course for Anna's rehabilitation with hopes of discharge sometime in July. It seemed almost too good to believe and a little bit scary, too, after the security of her excellent care in both hospitals.

Drs. Rob Hanson and Janet Mueller were still at Children's, now as her big brother and sister. The night they became engaged, they headed straight for Anna's room to share the good news with her. Anna was thrilled; how she loved those dear ones!

Dr. Dipersio often walked over from Barnes to check on her, too. Of course, Dr. Jim, or "Dr. Ab" as he was nicknamed, continued to pop in by divine appointment every time we needed advice or encouragement.

As Anna's walking skills progressed, she graduated from quad cane to a stick cane and began the laborious feat of stairs. If she was to be discharged to Grandmother's house, she wanted to maneuver stairs and sleep in a twin bed near the boys in our temporary quarters there. When school started, she hoped to walk to classes at Westminster Academy. It was a Herculean effort, but her resolve was strong.

Occupational therapists worked on life skills such as strength and coordination in her hands to eat, brush her teeth, and dress herself. Socks were the hardest! They were also very hard for Mama to leave alone for the struggling learner.

Dr. Robin Park, pediatric psychiatrist and Parkway sister, spent several lunchtimes with Anna alone, both as a friend and for clinical psychological assessment. She regarded Anna as amazingly sound and secure through it all. We also knew that Robin faithfully prayed for us. She was another of God's special blessings.

We continued collecting pictures of ideas for the house we hoped the Lord would provide soon for our family. Our house in Texas had now been rebuilt from the fire and was on the market. Each month *Better Homes and Gardens* was carefully perused, and a front door, pretty window treatment, or use of vintage quilts would be cut out and added to the manila folder prepared for that happily anticipated project.

Between and after therapy sessions Anna studied beginning algebra with the hospital's teacher, Miss Donna. We also completed American History.

When a new patient was admitted and feeling sad, the nurses often recruited Anna to make a personal visit to cheer them up, which she gladly accomplished. Some, like Kara, became teammates. Kara's mom later sent word that when Kara was confirmed as a Roman Catholic, she took the Christian name "Anna." Another little African American preschooler, a kidney patient, used to slip out of her room at night, trot down the hall and push Anna's door open, then scoot up into my lap or sleeping cot. Anna would laugh and beep the nurses' station to report that she was AWOL again.

Barnes Hospital's Bone Marrow Transplant Unit celebrated 1000 transplants with an extravagant gala evening at the Frontenac Hilton, and Anna was invited with special permission to attend. Since Dwight and Joshua were in Wyoming on a youth mission, Dr. Lori Kutka offered to help and accompany us. With happy determination, Anna dressed in her best dress and we drove to the hotel. Using every ounce of energy, she made it to our table in the very back of the ballroom where the program had already begun. It was a lovely event in every detail.

As the evening's highlight, the master of ceremonies recognized each adult transplant survivor present. As names were called, survivors stood and walked to the front of the beautifully decorated ballroom to stand together on platform risers as a group. Names were read in alphabetical order, but Anna's name was skipped. That seemed odd and disappointing, but we chalked it up to uncertainty about her condition and the fact that she was now at Children's. Then, at the very end, after all the names were read, a special word and description of Anna was shared. To thunderous applause and a standing ovation from survivors, families, and the medical staff, Anna stood with help and then, leaning only on her little silver cane, slowly walked all by herself to the front of the cheering crowd. Her nurses cried. Me, too.

We learned that Dr. Hanna Khoury had written a professional research paper for medical colleagues around the world about Anna's stupendous comeback from aspergillosis. Knowledge gained through her experience and treatment would now be available to help other patients in what had previously seemed a hopeless situation.

Wednesday, July 3 was set to be the big day—discharge! All efforts from Anna's team targeted that day. She diligently pursued therapy, continuing to work hard and also enjoying celebration at every turn.

Speech and occupational therapists took her out to lunch where the final exam was to order her own food and make a purchase with her own money. She bought a candle for me labeled "Home Sweet Home."

Norma and Norman Lockett hosted a Father's Day Tex-Mex luncheon, all homemade, Anna's favorite, in their home for which she was granted a special two-hour "pass."

Her teacher, Miss Donna, brought her a bronzed medal of "Winged Victory" inscribed on the back:

7–3-96

ANNA

YOU WON

Anna clutched it and beamed. I cried.

On Tuesday Shelly and Debra organized an all day "open house" for everyone at Children's or Barnes who had ever been a part of Anna's care. Cake and punch and homemade goodies were set up for the celebration.

Kay Quinn from Channel 5 News came to interview Anna for their third story about her. Anna smiled into the camera and shared from her heart sincere thanks for God's grace to her and the help of so many dedicated caregivers. When asked what her goal would be now, she quickly responded that she was eager to get back to life with her brothers. She also wanted people to know that no matter how bad things might get, there was always hope.

That night after everyone had gone, we readied for bed and prayers. This one hospital stay had been more than eight months, thirteen months since Anna was first admitted to Children's Hospital, unit 9 West, room 44 (soon afterward), the very room she now occupied and would leave the following morning. Such a long haul, and now it would finally end.

With all sincerity, Anna looked into my eyes and said, "You know, Mom, I never would have asked for any of this; but it's really been a great year, hasn't it?"

A great year? By whose standards?

By Anna's.

It was a great year because she had known the love and support of so many good people. Because she had experienced fully the grace of God. And because, in spite of everything, hope had prevailed.

We hugged tightly and I agreed.

The next morning Dwight and Josh and Jonathan finished loading remaining stuff from Anna's room, discharge papers were officially signed, and it was time to go.

Waving and cheering, patients and staff lined the hallway as Anna, on her cane, made her way down the hall. Her Texas A&M tee-shirt could have been Miss America's gown. A wheelchair was offered but nicely refused. No, thank you. Not this time. Her little cane was enough.

Down the elevator, through the lobby, and out the automatic glass doors. Even the front desk clerks and security attendants knew Anna. Good-byes and blessings continued all the way. Daddy had pulled our white "Mama bus" to the curb and was waiting. Josh and Jonathan helped her in, closed the sliding door, and, at last, we were off.

Anna arrived "home" with great joy and contentment shared by all of us to be together as a family again, even under Grandmother's roof instead of our own. Lord, bless her for it. We will always be grateful.

Josh and Jonathan listed favorite menu requests and kept Mom running to the grocery market and back in the kitchen. We laughed and ate and retold a thousand "remember when" stories. Anna relished the boisterous love and fellowship of her brothers.

Every night she quietly, laboriously climbed the stairs to sleep in a little bed only a few feet between her brothers' bed and the one I thankfully shared with Dwight for the first time in many moons. We could all hear each other breathe, and after "lights out" could count on repeated "Good-nights" from one to another. Anna felt safe and complete in that upstairs cocoon for which she had so longed. In the morning she would make her way down the stairs and remain down until bedtime again. It worked.

Returns to the hospital for outpatient therapy three times a week were not too popular, so we discovered reward treats like drive-throughs for St. Louis ice cream custard. Miss Linda resumed school catch-up studies through the homebound program.

The Davises came from Texas and Anna insisted that she was able to navigate the St. Louis Arch and Union Station.

Teen-age girls from Parkway, ready to welcome Anna into their circle, put together "girls night out," bringing taco ingredients, fruit pizza, and the classic movie, "An Affair to Remember." When it ended, I smiled that all of them were sniffing like their grandmothers had when the movie was first made.

As promised a year before, Dwight bought tickets to The Muny for the musical "Sleeping Beauty" coming up the following week. Josh and Jonathan declined. Anna could hardly wait.

There were ten wonderful days.

Sunday morning at one o'clock and again at three, Anna coughed. I gave her cough medicine and was concerned, but she felt cool and wanted to go back to sleep.

At six o'clock an alarming croup-like breathing sounded like a loud train. It was terrible; she gasped for every breath. I woke Dwight and called Dr. Janet Mueller at home who ordered an ambulance to begin oxygen immediately and get to the hospital.

Anna adamantly opposed both telephone calls and especially returning to the hospital. She managed to gasp, "I'm. . . not. . . sick."

In the scarce light of dawn, the ambulance came pealing down the gravel lane, lights and siren wailing. When the paramedics walked in, Anna insisted on wearing her A&M athletic shoes and making her own way down the stairs, but by the bottom step she willingly acquiesced to their stretcher.

Her breathing improved after getting oxygen, but x-rays at Children's Hospital showed irregularities in her lungs. She was soon moved from the emergency room up to 9 West and that afternoon transferred to Barnes Hospital 13100, the bone marrow unit. We were back in the hospital.

SHADOWS

A little oxygen support with nasal prongs and Anna felt better, except for disappointment at being incarcerated again. At least she was back on the familiar unit with her dear nurses. To cheer her up, they ordered pizza delivered to her room and goaded her with corny Aggie jokes.

Her immediate concern was the Muny tickets for Tuesday evening. She explained to Dr. Dipersio that she just couldn't stay in the hospital. It was the Muny! Her good friend, unable to say "yes" but reluctant to say "no," settled for "We'll see."

One testing option, a bronchoscopy, would look down with a scope into Anna's lungs and see what was going on there. Dr. Dipersio explained that this invasive procedure had its risks but could provide the most definitive information. Although hesitant to put her through the ordeal, he felt it might be necessary. After prayer and careful consideration, the test was scheduled for Wednesday.

Anna won her consolation prize, permission to go to the Muny Tuesday evening. "Happy" is an understatement.

It was a beautiful, clear evening. We left with strict instructions that Anna must take oxygen along "just in case," and that if she felt even a little sick, we would return immediately. Arrangements were made for special parking next to the entrance, and folding chairs for Dwight and me were set up on either side of her wheelchair in an open space with a great view of the stage. Perfect. In the background we could see the towering buildings of Washington University Medical Center, Barnes and Children's Hospitals.

Singing, orchestra, and costumes were delightful, and no one appreciated this performance more than one little girl in the wheelchair. When the plump fairy godmother appeared in her gaudy emerald green ballgown, Anna whispered to me in innocent wonder, "Isn't she beautiful?" Her Daddy and I watched her more than the musical and thanked God for every precious minute.

Afterward, back in her hospital room, Dr. Dipersio, whom Anna had long before nicknamed "the night owl," came in. "So, how was it?"

Anna bubbled over with every detail of her special evening. She had not needed oxygen at all and was breathing fine. He studied her and debated. "Maybe you don't need that test tomorrow after all." But the decision had already been made.

Next morning's bronchoscopy confirmed with cultures a diagnosis of para influenza, the virus of infants that causes croup. Since Anna's resistance was greatly diminished, similar to a newborn baby's, what might have appeared in other people as a common cold became a serious problem for her lungs.

Since she would remain asleep from anesthesia most of the afternoon, Dwight left early with hugs and kisses and promises to see us the next day. We were in the room right next to the nurses' station equipped with monitors and gadgets used for intensive care. This troubled me, but the nurses assured us they just wanted Anna nearby; but, since she was there, they would go ahead and track her on the monitors, which relayed automatically to their main desk.

As Anna slept, I sat next to her bed mesmerized by the monitor, intent on every breath and heartbeat. Late that night she still had not awakened and I was still watching, when her oxygen saturation level began to drop, one point after another.

Before the alarm sounded at the nurses' desk, I stood there asking for assistance. Nurse Bonita took one look and immediately snapped into action, calling for others who hurried in to help and asked me to step into the hall. Moving quickly toward the small waiting room to call Dwight, I was surprised to find deacon Charlie already there, prompted without our knowledge to come and pray.

Anna was skillfully intubated (placed on a ventilator "breathing machine") and whisked away to the Barnes medical intensive care unit, one of the few places we had not been before.

From the journal:

FRIDAY, JULY 19
We are told there are only thirty documented cases of para influenza in bone marrow transplant patients. A paper on it has been copied and placed in Anna's chart. The prognosis is very poor for her, but the Lord is good. She is in His hands now as always. This is yet another episode of the "impossible" for Anna.

I have wondered why God is allowing Anna to be struck down again in this terrible way. There are at least four possibilities:

This is His judgment for sin in our lives, and He is bringing us to repentance.

He is allowing us to be tested, like Job, never apart from His faithfulness. He monitors every step.

He is using us here in the lives of others as encouragement or even example.

He is now laying the foundation for a greater future work, which we cannot see.

SATURDAY, JULY 20

Anna had a rough night but has been more stable today. The BMT nurses and Dwight collaborated to arrange a three thousand dollar nap for me in the intensive care room on 13100. I showered and changed clothes, too. Feel like a new woman. Bless them. While I was resting, Dwight sustained rocky waves with Anna. It's wonderful to have him here.

She is receiving Ribavirin treatments every day for several hours. This is a very toxic drug, the reason we are here instead of on the BMT floor. It must be administered in a negative pressure room so it cannot get into air ducts, etc. The machine is hooked up to Anna's ventilator so that it goes through the tube in her mouth directly to her lungs. We are not allowed in her room during treatment because of the poison, but are allowed back in when the treatment is finished.

The respiratory technician, nurse, and doctors wear goggles, special extra-protection masks, gloves, and gowns, all of which are disposed of when they leave and new ones used if they re-enter. I wonder, if it is that dangerous and potent, how it may affect Anna's lungs. It is ordinarily prescribed for three days, but the doctors have ordered it on Anna for seven to ten days. Lord, deliver it to exactly the right spot and give us patience to wait.

(Later, back with Anna in her cubicle.)

Many people have in various ways communicated to us the inspiration Channel 5's latest news story was for them, especially the repeated emphasis on "miracle" and the anchorman's comment following the clip at ten o'clock that "It was Anna's faith in God that saw her through."

Beth Ann called from Texas. She and Sue and Mel were to come on Monday for a few days for Bethie's birthday. She loves Anna and is bewildered and afraid at this turn of events. I shared with her that the very best thing for Anna would be Heaven. It would be bad for me and bad for Bethie and bad for the rest of the world who would miss the blessing of her life, but it would be stunningly best for Anna.

As I attempt to sit calmly in my chair next to the wall in this tiny cubicle, Anna's oxygen saturation level drops and rises and drops some more in decrescendo pattern.

I pray, quote Scripture, and even bash the powers of Satan in silence as the room fills with doctors and nurses—seven by head count besides Anna and me. It is a restrained cacophony as they debate in hushed, intense voices what is happening, why, and what to do now. If I rise from the chair, they may send me out and not let me back in. I remain still and quiet but do not budge.

Oxygen percentage is bumped to a hundred per cent. "That's toxic," one says. The nurse adjusts the vent tube, then suctions. The ICU resident pauses beside me and casually asks, "Will your husband be coming back soon?" I hesitate only a moment before stepping outside the wall of glass doors to call Grandmother's house. She will tell him. He should be on his way soon.

79, 78, 76, 74, 74, 74, 75, 76, 76, finally, agonizingly snail-paced, it gets to 80.

It should be 90 minimum, 95 to 100 preference. Come on, baby girl. Breathe on her, breath of God. Fill her with life anew.

What a paradox as I contemplate the joy of Heaven for her and in the next second quake in near terror at the thought of losing her. This is the brink at which others have stood—the vast multitude of humankind, one at a time, over a thousand generations.

They have written it and told it, but at this moment it is a brand new phenomenon, for I have never been here before.

I'm in the waiting room, gently ousted from the presence of the orderly commotion in Anna's ICU cubicle. The Ribavirin treatment is about to begin, an hour and a half late. Instead of one respiratory tech, there are four. Anna lies motionless, my beloved child, and I the mother depart, the gulf between us two silent partners filled with gifted, skilled medical laborers whose training and doctor titles are now put to the real test. So is mine. Now I wait.

"They that wait upon the Lord shall renew their strength. They shall mount up with wings as eagles. They shall run and not be weary, they shall walk and not faint" Isaiah 40:31.

"I would have despaired unless I had believed that I would see the goodness of the Lord in the land of the living. Wait for the Lord; Be strong, and let your heart take courage; Yes, wait for the Lord" Psalm 27:13–14.

"My soul, wait thou only upon God; for my expectation is from Him. He only is my rock and my salvation; He is my defense; I shall not be moved" Psalm 62:5–6.

PM–LATE

Anna's heart (pulse), blood pressure, and saturation are all perfect. She is resting peacefully while receiving the Ribavirin. What made the difference?

Nurse Jan told me they started Ativan continuous drip for better sedation. Good.

Dwight told me tonight that Jonathan fasted and prayed today.

Thank You, Lord.

Physically worn but encouraged. I believe God is at work even though the prognosis remains grim.

Janet and Rob came over yesterday afternoon and said at morning worship (Parkway) young children, teen-agers, adults, and senior citizens filled the front altar and prayed for Anna. This morning's x-ray showed slight improvement in the right lung.

Dr. Tebas from Infectious Disease said she is really no better. Dr. Dipersio came in while Jonathan and I were downstairs for dinner and told Dwight he is very sorry but he just doesn't think she can make it.

Dr. Dipersio was out of town Wednesday when Anna was intubated and Thursday when we moved to the MICU. Friday he came by late in the afternoon, very solemn.

This is Anna's official physician of record, also the chief of bone marrow transplants.

The first time our family met the great doctor, he candidly said we should pray to "he, she, or it, or whatever you think it might be," if it would make us feel better.

As he sat quietly in Anna's little cubicle in the ICU Friday, we could hear the steady rhythm of the ventilator whooshing pumped breaths into her diseased lungs, her sweet sleeping face almost hidden behind a maze of tubes and wires. The scientist/physician, now our friend, said simply, "I prayed for Anna today."

Surely God of Heaven and earth heard his heart's cry as he turned to Him in behalf of this angel child. I long for Anna to know what he said. Only a few weeks ago at Children's Hospital after prayers (Anna always prays by name at night for Dr. Dipersio, Therese, Shelly, and Davida), she wept, tears running down her cheeks, saying if Dr. Dipersio didn't turn to God, she would not see him in Heaven.

Lord, our Father, please hear them both.

Jonathan is here tonight. We played Scrabble and he will sleep here in the waiting room chairs with us while Anna receives Ribavirin treatment. He and Josh came yesterday afternoon with Carol and Phil to see their sister for the first time this trip.

It was traumatic for them to see her on a ventilator, but that was their choice. Her kidneys are having a hard time, and the extra fluid (three liters ahead) makes her puffy.

Our nurse, Susan, was there to explain her condition and treatment and to answer their questions.

WEDNESDAY, JULY 23

Bless the Lord, Anna is better. Creatinine is 1.4 today (1.8 yesterday, 2.1 day before), so kidneys are better. 02 is at 50% (21% is normal for us), and she is initiating most breaths. The ventilator is set for fourteen breaths per minute and she is taking eighteen. Peep level has been turned down from seven to five (pressure of air forced by ventilator into lungs to open the alveoli). No fever. Last Ribavirin treatment is tonight and she has tolerated them all.

Dr. Tebas (infectious disease) said this morning when (not if) she is over this, she should pick up right where she left off two weeks ago. Dr. Castro and his team (pulmonary) were also encouraging that she is on the way back.

Dr. Dipersio came again late last night, nurse Nancy said. I was napping in the chair.

Dr. Hanna Khoury shared this story with us the other day:

When the Shah of Iran was still in power, he went out one day to hunt wild pigs. While he was hunting, a wild pig charged toward him. A poor farmer stood nearby, observing; he quickly shot the pig, saving the Shah. The Shah, overwhelmed with gratitude, said to the man, "You have saved my life; now I must repay you. Tell me anything you wish, and I will do it for you."

The peasant replied, "I have need of nothing."

The Shah insisted, "But I must reward you for saving my life. Please tell me something you desire."

Unchanged, the poor man answered, "Shah, there is nothing more I wish. I have a good life as a farmer."

The Shah brightened. "Ah! You are a farmer! You will come to my palace and be my gardener and be cared for the rest of your life."

So, the peasant moved to the Shah's palace in Teheran and became his gardener.

Ten years later, one day the gardener came running breathlessly up to the Shah.

"Shah! Shah! Ten years ago I saved your life, and now you must save mine."

"Of course," came the immediate response. "What do you need? "

"I must borrow your fastest horse."

"You have it. But why do you need my horse?"

"I was just in the garden working, and behind a bush I saw Death. Now I must escape from him as quickly as possible to a faraway place. If you give me your horse, I can go to Samarcand (city) and from there to Turkey."

"Very well," the Shah agreed. "Go in peace."

The gardener sped away at a furious gallop, and the Shah turned and walked to the garden. Sure enough, there behind a bush was Death.

"Death," said the Shah. "What are you doing here? Why have you frightened my gardener? He is a good gardener and has been with me for ten years."

"I'm sorry, Shah," Death replied. "I did not mean to frighten him. I was just surprised to see him here. I'm supposed to meet him in Samercand in four days."

SATURDAY, JULY 27

Anna is no worse and her x-rays have slightly improved. She has a fever and nurse Lisa has drawn cultures.

Since Ribavirin treatments ended, I can stay here in the cubicle all the time. Some of the nurses and church people see me as a martyr and keep trying to persuade me to leave her for some sleep. The truth is that I need to be here with her for my own peace as well as for her.

She is now semi-conscious. Although she doesn't open her eyes, she does often respond with eyebrows and nods. Her arms are in soft restraints strapped to the rails, but there is enough slack for her to raise her hand with outstretched fingers for me to hold and bring back down to her side. I stroke her hair and gently remind her to relax and breathe slowly or let the machine do it for her. I wipe her with damp washcloths or fan her using a big piece of sterile cardboard or sing the old hymns we both love. Sometimes we read aloud, Scripture or the quaint stories of Grace Livingston Hill.

Lots of visitors come by from the hospital community, both Children's and Barnes, who have grown to love Anna during the past year. Their badges give them ICU access, and the nurses here are frankly amazed at the constant flow toward her cubicle.

One louder than usual dialogue outside our curtain was the voice of one of Anna's orderlies from last year arguing with her nurse. "That's my baby in there, and I'm going in!"

I peeked out and invited him in. He stood at the foot of Anna's bed and tried to keep from crying when he saw her. Remembering that Anna was a track runner, he had gone to considerable trouble to collect personal notes and pictures for her from Gail Devers and Jackie Joyner-Kersee, who will compete next week in Olympic track and field finals. I hope Anna will be awake to watch them on television.

We need another miracle, according to "Dr. Ab," Jim Fleshman. I don't know how many our quota allows but do know that the Lord's pockets are very deep.

It's hard to understand why He would miraculously and magnificently intervene to heal her before, and then so quickly allow her to be here at death's door again. That is similar to Peter's experience I read about this morning in Acts 5.

Peter and the other apostles with him were imprisoned for the cause of Christ, v. 18; then, in the next verse, an angel of the Lord during the night opened the gates of the prison, releasing them with the command to "Go your way, stand and speak to the people in the temple the whole message of this Life."

They did exactly as the Lord commanded. Their obedience took them back to the temple where they were arrested again, taken before the Council, and because of the wise counsel of Gamaliel, instead of death they were sentenced to flogging (traditionally thirty-nine lashes). For *this,* I ask, they were miraculously freed?

Verse 41 is a jewel: "So they went on their way from the presence of the Council, rejoicing that they had been considered worthy to suffer shame for His name."

Some time ago I had written a note of reminder in the margin at this passage. Many years after this instance, when Peter was an old man, he wrote in I Peter 4:14–16,

"If you are reviled for the name of Christ, you are blessed . . . if anyone suffers as a Christian, let him not feel ashamed, but in that name let him glorify God."

As I review Peter's testimony today, it is verse 19 that gives strength and encouragement to a mother's heart: "Therefore, let those also who suffer according to the will of God entrust their souls to a faithful Creator in doing what is right" I Peter 4:19.

Lord, our Creator and Master, give me grace to entrust my soul and that of my beloved child to Your faithful care.

MONDAY, JULY 29

Anna's blood pressure and oxygen saturation dropped, even with 100% oxygen. Nurses, doctors, and respiration techs worked with her as I prayed. Dwight came with the boys and so did Sue and Mel and Bethie. Her already heavy sedation was increased dramatically to insure a deep sleep requiring minimum heart and lung activity. Her condition is grave.

Sue and Mel took the boys to dinner at Union Station; Dwight and I sat by Anna's bed and waited. Church members gathered in the waiting room to pray. The Youngs got a room in Queenie Tower and Mel sat with us till into the wee hours of the morning. What faithful friends.

Yesterday morning Mel stayed with Dwight while I went with Sue to their room to shower, stopping on 13100 to tell the nurses that Anna had made the night. Back into the ICU, we found Dr. Azah waiting in Anna's cubicle. He was not smiling and Dwight had tears in his eyes.

Sue and Bethie remained with Dwight as I moved outside with Viveck to hear the latest report: Fever still up—also white count, indicating a mysterious "super infection" apparently impervious to the bombardment of multiple broad spectrum antibiotics. The AM x-ray was much worse, both lungs completely white. Her condition was critical. Hope was diminishing by the hour.

The ICU attending physician and other specialists came in on their days off to perform a "mini bronch" through the ventilator tube. Afterward, the pulmonologist stayed with Anna for three hours. Everyone was obviously giving 100%.

All smears and cultures came back *negative*. The goal is to continue to support her through this in every way, monitoring all body systems, and hope for a turn-around.

WEDNESDAY, JULY 31

My pen seems to be losing some oomph. Looks like it may exactly be sufficient for the pages left in this journal, like God's grace for whatever a day brings.

Anna remains stable, intentionally paralyzed and heavily sedated, pulse and blood pressure slightly elevated. About 3:00 this morning she took a huge dip. A STAT x-ray was ordered to see if a lung had collapsed. A couple of nurses gathered to pray, and Bonita came down from 13100. Dwight was at youth camp with the boys. In half an hour she stabilized, lung x-ray was good, and we all settled down again.

ICU doctor asked if I would mind praying with some of the other families of patients in the unit.

SATURDAY MORNING, AUGUST 3

Last night was the best night we have had, no major alarms or dips. Visitors are not allowed in the ICU overnight, so it is a great favor to Anna and me that they still allow me to stay with her in a chair next to the wall.

Nurse Jane from 13100 brought a delicious supper last night, all homemade: seafood salad, marinated cucumbers, fresh tomatoes, crackers and cheese, and chocolate chip cookies. She made cookies early in the week and sent with the boys to youth camp.

So glad they are back–kind of like to keep our wagons in a circle these days.

Keep going back to the Psalms for comfort and encouragement as we continue to wait.

Psalm 124–"Had it not been the Lord who was on our side . . . then they would have swallowed us alive. . . then the waters would have engulfed us, the stream would have swept over our soul; then the raging waters would have swept over our soul. Blessed be the name of the Lord. Our help is in the name of the Lord, Who made heaven and earth."

Psalm 125–"Those who trust in the Lord are as Mt. Zion, which cannot be moved, but abides forever. As the mountains surround Jerusalem, so the Lord surrounds His people from this time forth and forever."

Psalm 126–"Those who sow in tears shall reap with joyful shouting. He who goes to and fro weeping, carrying his bag of seed, shall indeed come again with a shout of joy, bringing his sheaves with him."

Psalm 127–"Unless the Lord builds the house, they labor in vain who build it; unless the Lord guards the city, the watchman keeps awake in vain. . . For He gives to His beloved, even in his (her/Anna's) sleep."

Psalm 128–"How blessed is everyone who fears the Lord, who walks in His ways. When you shall eat of the fruit of your hands, you will be happy and it will be well with you. Your wife shall be like a fruitful vine within your house, your children like olive plants around your table."

Psalm 129–"The blessing of the Lord be upon you; we bless you in the name of the Lord."

Psalm 130–"Out of the depths I have cried to Thee, O Lord. Lord, hear my voice! Let Thine ears be attentive to my supplications. If Thou, O Lord, shouldst mark iniquities, O Lord, who could stand? But there is forgiveness with Thee, that Thou mayest be feared."

"I wait for the Lord, my soul does wait, and in His Word do I hope. My soul waits for the Lord more than the watchmen for the morning; indeed, more than the watchmen for the morning. O Israel (Sherry Ann), hope in the Lord; for with the Lord there is lovingkindness, and with Him is abundant redemption. And He will redeem Israel from all his iniquities."

Psalm 131–"O Lord, my heart is not proud, or my eyes haughty; nor do I involve myself in great matters, or in things too difficult for me. Surely I have composed and quieted my soul; like a weaned child rests against his mother, my soul is like a weaned child within me. O Israel (Sherry Ann), hope in the Lord from this time forth and forever."

MONDAY, AUGUST 5

Still waiting and watching. "Watch and pray," Jesus instructed His apostles in the greatest crunch of all time, in the Garden of Gethsemanae. That is His call to me for these days.

WEDNESDAY, AUGUST 7

Still waiting. The Lord is faithful. Alan Brooks just came by. Today's lung x-ray is better than yesterday's. Thank You.

FRIDAY, AUGUST 9

Sitting beside Anna's bed in the ICU–watching and praying. Yesterday was the much dreaded tracheotomy, but honestly it was the best thing for her. The trach is another good example of the Scriptural principle, "In a multitude of counsel there is safety." All the docs and nurses agreed it would be the best thing for Anna, and they were right.

It's good to see her sweet face without that big blue apparatus coming out of it. Her hair is thick and curly, like copper ringlets around her angel face. A few times she has partially opened her eyes and reached out her hand to me. Once when I told her I loved her, her little lips moved in silence—"I love you." Thank You, Father.

Dwight will probably come later. He and the boys went to a Cardinal game last night; the weather was perfect. Seems impossible that they will be in high school, another step toward manhood. They are exceptional young men in every way, rare treasures to their mother's heart.

SATURDAY MORNING, AUGUST 10

Anna is having a thoracic CT scan. She began to de-sat late last night and her blood pressure dropped while pulse and temperature escalated. Her condition steadily deteriorated, but I kept hesitating to call Dwight in case he should be awakened and then her condition reverse for the better. He and the boys had come by for a few minutes on their way to the Rams pre-season football game and I knew it would be very late when they got home. Anna's nurse Lea Ann agreed we could wait. At 6:30 I called him to please come, and just a minute after putting the telephone down, Lea Ann came in suggesting I should call him to come. It's been a long night of tension and no sleep; a little fuzzy.

3:30—afternoon. CT scan confirmed the x-rays: both lungs intact. The unanimous consensus is that she has full-flown sepsis, systemic infection throughout her body—very serious, particularly in conjunction with ARDS. Blood pressure is stable. Pulse has slowed. Temperature is down. The Lord is good.

Yesterday I wrote "thank you" notes, twenty in all, and needed stamps to mail them. When Dwight brought in today's mail, there was a note from Mrs. Riggs in Texas with stamps enclosed. Twenty.

SUNDAY EVENING, AUGUST 11

Once again the Lord has been gracious to deliver Anna. This afternoon her oxygen saturation went down and her pulse went up again. Her condition deteriorated with brilliant caring medical professionals all around her bed yearning to help, yet helpless.

Dwight was here, too. We prayed and watched through the glass. They gave her paralyzing drugs again, assuring me that she is adequately sedated and will not be frightened. A new triple lumen catheter was inserted next to the A line for much needed IV access. Her medications and sedations are now very complicated. I kissed her feet, knelt by her bed and prayed when a spot became vacant.

There was so much clatter and commotion and chatter, even as they struggled to make her sleep. The children have never been accustomed to such noise ever. I gently reminded them one at a time to lower their voices, "Use your quietest indoor voice, please." They kindly quieted down though still aggressively pursuing everything they knew to do—another lung x-ray to see if it was deflated, an EKG to check for a possible heart attack, many trial-and-error variations with the ventilator. I found myself beside her, left hand resting on her curly head, right hand on her arm, softly singing the old hymns only she could hear.

Since the monitor and clock were behind me, they ceased to be our focus. I don't know how long, many stanzas later, Dr. Alan Brooks smiled faintly and said, "It's better. I think she's stable." A little while later he added in his South African accent, "That was scary."

Josh and Jonathan came in while all that was going on. Josh stepped up next to me and stood with his hand on my shoulder, so dear. People from the church are gathered in the waiting room to pray. I went out for a moment to thank them. Anna's blood pressure remains stable (with medication to pump it up), 02 saturation is up to 95%, pulse is down to 120, and carbon dioxide is down to 37.

I asked Dwight to stay with us tonight and he agreed. Think he's gone to get a change of clothes—still had his Sunday suit on. It is a real comfort to have him here with us this evening. I know God gives us the grace we need for every situation. I did not have the grace to give her up this afternoon, and it was not His appointed time to take her.

It's 9:05 PM. Still watching and praying. At Dr. Randy Brown's suggestion, yesterday we hung the poster of Anna preparing to run track on the wall over the head of her bed. I wrote out Psalm 27:14 and taped it beside the picture, "Wait for the Lord; Be strong and let your heart take courage; Yes, wait for the Lord."

How many times those words have been repeated. They are burned into my soul.

"Wait for the Lord."

TUESDAY, AUGUST 13

Dr. Powderly, Irish, Infectious Disease, now old friend who helped us through the aspergillus ordeal in November, told us gravely that Anna needs another miracle. She has remained stable since Sunday's scare but is on maximum ventilator support.

Yesterday afternoon I was reading some of the Psalms to her and came to Psalm 40, which begins, "I waited patiently for the Lord, and He inclined to me and heard my cry."

Not "inclined His ear" but inclined His whole self to me. Body language shows our attention. I have His full attention when I cry out to Him.

It finishes, "Since I am afflicted and needy, let the Lord be mindful of me; Thou art my help and my deliverer; Do not delay, O my God."

So much of that Psalm is special for this setting. Verse 2, "He brought me up out of the miry clay, and set my feet on a rock."

Things seem to be better, then we sink again in the mire; but through it all, He is our rock, our firm foundation.

Verse 3, "He put a new song in my mouth, a song of praise to our God."

We have always laughed about my terrible singing voice, but Anna has always loved for me to sing hymns to her. I am more than a little embarrassed to sing with other people around, but it is the one thing I can do for her. It's certainly not for "show." Same thing with prayer. I was shy about praying on my knees in the ICU cubicle, lest it be interpreted as a Pharisee type display, but then the Lord gently nudged me back to my knees, where I am praying to Him alone.

The last half of verse 3 about the song of praise to God says, "Many will see and fear, and will trust in the Lord." Emphasis is not that bystanders "hear" the song but "see" it. They will trust in the Lord because they are able to see the living witness.

THURSDAY, AUGUST 15

Dwight read Matthew 18:10 today. Jesus said, "See that you do not despise one of these little ones, for I say to you, that their angels in heaven continually behold the face of My Father who is in Heaven."

What a beautiful reminder that Anna's angels are even now on duty. Even though we do not see them (to our knowledge), they are busy doing the Lord's bidding on her behalf. Thank You, Father.

Her condition is still very critical, yet somewhat more stable—no fever, kidney function improved, blood pressure stable without medication. Dr. Kollef, ICU director, pointed out today, very emphatically, that while those things sound good, the main life or death issue now is her lungs, which he thinks are worse. ARDS makes them stiff, inflexible. The ventilator is now giving maximum support with no improvement in her oxygen saturation levels.

In the last few days I have again given Anna back to God, tearfully but confidently assured that His will for her is the best, and that may be Heaven very soon. I have told her that if Jesus asks her to come with Him, she must turn loose of Mama's hand and take His hand and go with Him to Heaven. She will never be alone. It won't be scary, because Jesus will be taking her there. I don't know exactly what it's like, except that it is wonderful. That's a promise. Daddy and the boys and I will be there soon, and then it will be permanent—no more separation ever.

I have shared with Josh and Jonathan what I told their sister. I tried to assure the boys that if it is God's will for Anna to go to Heaven now, her passage will be gentle—peacefully asleep here, only to wake up in Heaven. We gathered around her bed and Dwight prayed, thanking God for Anna and pledging our family's love for her and devotion to God's great will and purpose.

The Bible says Hezekiah, King of Israel, called out to God on his deathbed for deliverance. God gave him a reprieve of fifteen years, and then it was time to go.

Maybe God's purpose all along has been for Anna to go on to Heaven, but in response to our prayers and desperate need He graciously and miraculously extended her dear life for another year, allowing me cherished memories of this unique time alone with her. Maybe He knew that I just really couldn't give her up last year, and so He gave us this year to prepare for separation from each other.

She amazed me just before leaving Children's Hospital July 3 by saying, without any provocation, "You know, Mom, I never would have asked for any of this, but it's really been a good year."

I almost felt a tingle as she said that and do now as I vividly picture her shining eyes and sincere countenance as she said it. What a kid. She lost most of her possessions in the fire. She lost her friends in Texas, moving in the night to a Missouri hospital without even saying "good-bye." She lost her Dad and brothers for a big part of the year. She lost the ability to read, to use her hands, to walk. She even lost her beautiful red hair. Yet, in spite of all that, she could genuinely affirm, "You know, Mom, it's been a really good year."

Venna Davis sent me a cross-stitch kit last fall of Noah's Ark. I've been working on it all year at Anna's bedside. Ironically, she is now at this precarious point and the cross-stitch is almost finished. There is a quandary in my heart as I look over at the nearly completed project. When it is finished, will Anna's sickness be over, too, one way or the other? She has followed every stitch with such interest as the intricate design has gradually appeared on the blank fabric background. She's already claimed that when it is finished, it will be hers.

No real change except that the tube feeding during the night apparently went through her tummy with no residuals left when the nurse checked again. The two syringe-fulls should contribute essential nutrition that will allow some decrease in the TPN.

Again and again I repeat to my quivering heart, "Wait for the Lord; Be strong, and let your heart take courage; Yes, wait for the Lord."

My parents came yesterday. Dwight took them and the boys out to dinner, and when he returned late last night he had a plastic bag filled with cookies individually wrapped in napkins from Josh. I've been munching on them this morning with instant hot apple cider from Aunt Rachel.

Carol Ponceroli from occupational therapy popped in for a few minutes, then Derrick, one of the orderlies. There is almost a steady stream of visitors from the hospital community. It reminds me of Alba. Dwight and I began married life there in that little town, population 505, where everyone was a neighbor in the best sense of the word.

All of us walked to the tiny post office and asked Elwood for the mail, greeting friendly passersby on the way. What happy, golden days those were. They come to mind this morning.

It was a frightening midnight ride from East Texas to St. Louis a year ago, to the big city, to a huge hospital complex, so enormous it is the second largest employer in St. Louis, listed again this year in *U. S. News & World Report* as one of the top ten hospitals in the United States. We were suddenly immersed in a swarming throng of medical personnel, technical procedures, and metropolitan perspectives as foreign to Alba as the most opposite pole in the world.

Today, almost fifteen months later, when I walk downstairs to the cafeteria or over to Children's Hospital for a shower, it's actually a lot like Elwood's post office. Familiar faces smile and ask, "How's Anna today?" The people who are in and out of this tiny ICU cubicle throughout the day are no longer anonymous hospital employees but friends and neighbors. Dr. Trey Metford told us a few minutes ago he'll be rotating off the ICU service this Sunday, but he'll be back up to check on Anna. Dr. Hanna Khoury checks Anna's stats from his home computer and is here to see her every day. Nurse Theresa brought cherry tomatoes for my salad. We all had zucchini bread and cream cheese Cheryl Ferguson from our Parkway family brought in a pretty basket. The Lord is good.

Saturday morning Dwight called me over to the long narrow window in Anna's cubicle, pointing to a brilliant rainbow, grandly arched from heaven to earth, too splendid for words. The promise. God's sign of covenant. It was unquestionably from the Lord's own great hand for our heavy hearts, a magnificent *double* rainbow.

I raced out of the cubicle to find young Dr. Trey Metford, the ICU doc on duty. Following me to a nearby window, he gazed at it in wonder, too.

"Write it in her chart!" I said.

He looked back quizzically.

"Please write it in her chart," I insisted. "Please let Anna's medical record show that God sent a rainbow today."

Trey nodded in consent. "I will."

Death might separate us temporarily, but we would hold to God's promise that someday we would be together again in Heaven for eternity with Him.

A fresh, new journal—I picked it up in the gift shop downstairs some time ago. Into my mind pops the verse "This is the day which the Lord hath made; I will rejoice and be glad in it." ????? Rejoice? Be glad? As my cherished daughter, flesh of my flesh, lies before me on the brink of passage from this life?

"Rejoice in the Lord always"—"and," as if directed to my hesitation, "again I say, rejoice." Sounds like a command, even a gentle nudge. Need to study that word "rejoice." This is not a happy day, and the Lord does not require celebrating, but I know there is always a reason to say "thank you."

My eyes are swollen from tears shed after each visit from specialists following Anna. These are not interns and residents; they are senior attending physicians, faculty of this renowned Washington University Medical School facility, among the best in the country.

Dr. Braverman, cardiologist—Her heart sounds fine, yesterday's echocardiogram shows no problem. It's just her lungs now.

Dr. Powderly, infectious disease—No more apparent sepsis/infection. The problem now is her lungs.

Dr. Randy Brown, bone marrow transplant/hematology/oncology—here informally as her friend, since there's no more cancer. We will watch her for the next forty-eight hours, then talk again Monday. He keeps his head down, his voice low, then without a "good-bye" slips out through the floor length curtain that walls the front of our cubicle.

Dr. Kollef, pulmonologist and director of the Medical ICU (pronounced "mickew") told us this morning they are almost "out of rope." The damaged lungs have been scarred badly and despite maximum ventilation they are not allowing her to breathe effectively. One small possibility remains—experimental use of nitrous oxide to help open the lungs' avilli to receive the oxygen.

Dwight asked if Dr. Kollef knew of anyone who had recovered from a condition like Anna's using the nitrous oxide treatment, and he shook his head sadly, "No." He did say that it would "buy us some time." A little while ago they brought in a form for us to sign since it is experimental, and the respiratory techs brought in a large tank and attached it to the ventilator.

Almost immediately her 02 saturation on the monitor went up to 94%. Nurse Lisa said they would soon begin to wean her from the 100% oxygen from the ventilator, but ever since then her sats have been steadily dropping, so they have not been able to.

02 saturation is now 91%.

Dwight is here with us. He just stepped out to call the boys. We have prayed and prayed, seeking the Lord, pleading for our child. Lisa is suctioning residuals from the feeding tube; her feedings have not left her tummy.

Jim Fleshman has been our advocate and encourager throughout the last year. Every time things got hard, he would come back with a positive word. Now, he, too, is grave. "You can kick around the liver, you can even kick around the brain, but you can't kick around the lungs."

I still believe with all my heart that God can raise her up and give her a full, healthy, long life. As I "watch and pray," a kaleidoscope of picture memories crosses my mind: Preemie Anna in the NICU scooting around sideways in the isolette to prop her feet up above the round door.

Baby Anna—crawling to reach her brother's bottle for him.

Toddler Anna—sitting in the vanity sink facing the mirror while I, just behind her, am getting ready for the day. A little pretend powder and a ribbon for her hair, and she is ready, too.

I lift her up with a kiss on her curly top and she toddles behind me as we begin our day of housework and tending to the boys.

Birthday parties—most years together, some individual. "Birthday Olympics" at our house were their and their friends' favorites.

Christmas—the annual letter, decorated with Anna's drawings; a giant tree heavy with handmade ornaments, miniature gingerbread houses, family caroling at the nursing home, morning Bible verses from the advent calendar to count down days till the Baby Jesus ornament would be carefully placed. Anna's own wooden nativity set in her room, the only gift she asked for her ninth birthday. Santa's footprints leading from the front door to the tree where he always left a note and crumbs from Anna's cookies and milk. Anna's new dress, stitched by Mrs. Santa to match the one on her Christmas doll. No one delighted in our family's many traditions, decorations, and activities more than Anna. Once something made a memory, it was automatically a "tradition" and Anna remembered every one.

"Are you having a happy childhood?" How she and her brothers teased me about that question. It was sincere and they knew it—and used it! A few months ago she looked into my eyes from her hospital bed and said sincerely, "Mom, I want you to know I had a happy childhood."

The family post office—notes to one another carefully placed in the correct shoe box and later the antique wooden mailbox. Anna loved it best and used it most.

"Family Day"—in lieu of Halloween. Our very own family holiday just to celebrate each other. Excused absences from school and no work at church for Daddy.

It was our special day.

Teacher Luncheons at our house for each of their teachers. Anna led the boys in planning menus, making invitations, and decorating the dining table. Even now, when Carol helped her prepare lunch in occupational therapy for our family, the grilled cheese sandwiches and cookies had to be on pretty plates with handmade placecards decorated with stickers.

My reverie abruptly stops there. There were no more journal entries that evening. It was our last one together as a family here on earth. It seemed unreal. Anna was our Joy.

I remember the long, dark night, watching the monitor, still feeling the warmth of her soft skin, trying desperately to make every fleeting minute count.

So, we had come to this.

Usual conversation of medical staff in the unit was hushed. They moved about silently in and out of our cubicle and those of other patients. In the stillness of night, only the respirator's rhythm and clicks of monitors broke the silence.

Leaning over Anna's bed, stroking her hair, I whispered the hardest words of my life to her, "If Jesus comes tonight and asks you to go with Him, just turn loose of my hand and take His hand. It's the right thing to do."

Sweet Anna. Always the compliant, obedient child. At 8:45 AM she was gently, tenderly carried from earth to Heaven.

Anna was gone.

A week later, after the funeral, I picked up the journal and recorded Anna's passage from earth to Heaven.

From the journal

SATURDAY EVENING, AUGUST 24

Sunday, August 18, 1996, was the darkest day of my life, yet we were gently carried through it with the greatest of all grace of loving God. Josh, Jonathan, and Dwight were with us all night. Dwight and Jonathan napped in chairs in our cubicle; Josh came back and forth from the ICU waiting room where people from the church waited and prayed all night. He came into the cubicle about 3:00 AM and said, "Mom, if you'll close your eyes and sleep, I'll sit beside Anna and wake you up if you need to."

When the boys came earlier in the evening, around nine or ten, we gathered around Anna's bed, told her we loved her, prayed, sang some hymns, and Dwight and Jonathan read Scriptures aloud. We recounted favorite memories that brought smiles through our tears.

The nurses and doctors showed Anna and our family the greatest kindness and respect through those final hours. We will always be grateful to them. We also began composing Anna's memorial service–Scriptures, hymns, our pastor Bro. Lowrie, and also Dr. Jim since Ruby had prayed so faithfully.

We would ask Cheri to sing the Mallotte "Lord's Prayer" as she had sung it in our wedding. Anna always remembered lying in bed in Palestine as a little girl listening to Miss Cheri sing "The Lord's Prayer" late one Saturday night. The next morning she told us she thought she had heard the angels singing. Jonathan still remembered it, too.

In the pre-dawn hours as I sat by her hospital bed, knowing she would soon slip away from me and this life as we have known it, my heart ached for the child of my womb. My whole self yearned to hold her ravaged body next to mine and dare away death that would snatch her from me. The labyrinth of tubes and wires prevented such an embrace, but I continued to hold her hand and stroke her head until one of the nurses let down a rail and helped us as best she could.

Sometime during those hours I wrote out the obituary for the newspaper that would soon be necessary. I wanted to think through that carefully while the room was quiet. "Anna Joy Blankenship, beloved daughter of . . ." I was going to write in the journal, too, but while noting the date, the nurse came in and said it would be soon–that was probably around 6:00 AM. I woke Dwight and Jonathan, Josh returned, and for the next two and a half hours we treaded deep, dark waters, the whole time sustained by God's mercy, even as we trembled in the agony of those moments.

Finally the nurse came back in and turned off the monitors, but the ventilator continued pumping rhythmic breaths into the little chest that rose and fell in cadence.

In a moment or so, the ICU doc, Trey Metford, came in and stood silently.

"Is she gone?" we asked.

"I'm afraid so," he replied. "I need to check something first."

He checked her eyes, tried listening for her heart, then turned sadly to me.

"Mrs. Blankenship, Anna's in Heaven."

It was the dreaded moment we had hoped would never come.

Minutes and hours after that were like a dream. Someone told the waiting friends, and telephone calls began to go out relaying the news. Nurses called their compatriots on 13100 (bone marrow) and 9 West (Children's oncology).

I continued to hold the limp hand, which almost immediately turned white, as did her face, especially her lips. When the nurse removed her feeding tube, there was a faint sweet smile on Anna's beautiful face—no pain, no struggle. Sweet Granny always said there's a smile on your face when you see Jesus.

Jim Fleshman was with us through the late night and morning. He suggested the funeral home, and Dwight called to make necessary arrangements. Dwight took such good care of all those things.

I began to take down things on the walls—Anna's track poster, Scriptures, etc.—and gather the few belongings in the cubicle. There in the corner by the window propped her walking cane. What a bittersweet privilege, Anna's now still, lifeless form there beside me, to lift her little silver walking cane high in the air for the boys to see and to softly proclaim through my tears, "No more. No more."

How could I leave her? In my mind, I knew she had left, too, but the shell that was hers still lay in the hospital bed. One more touch.

Good people from the church were outside the ICU where they had kept vigil all night. We must thank them and receive their comfort. Tears flowed, but I must hold the sobs until we were safely in the car. Swallow hard. Deep breaths. More tears.

Three kind deacons promised to stay with Anna if I would leave her. God bless those three dear men. They were right. It was time to go. How would I ever leave? Minutes seemed like hours. Please, just one more look and touch. Precious, precious Anna. Flesh of my flesh.

Her brave, valiant struggle was over. Wails were just below the surface, but I would not cheapen her dignity with hysterics. Deep breath. Wipe my nose. More tears. It was time. Oh, Father, please help me.

By sheer will, I thanked the deacons, took one last loving look at Anna, my Joy, then turned and left with Dwight and Josh and Jonathan. There would be no going back.

RITUALS

From the Journal

MONDAY MORNING, AUGUST 26

Poor me. Poor, poor me. Poor us. Grateful that Anna is well and whole and happy today in Heaven, but poor, poor us without her.

Today is the first day of school. Last night we reviewed class schedules, labeled books and supplies, and laid out clothes. This morning I made sack lunches and we read Psalm 1 as Josh and Jonathan ate their cereal and bananas, characteristics of the "blessed man." I kissed all three men-folks good-bye at 6:45, finished cleaning the kitchen, then came up here and cried.

Anna's great desire was to go to school with her brothers this year, to graduate with them in the year 2000. They had little tee-shirts in kindergarten imprinted "Class of 2000." She loved school and always bubbled over at prospects of the first day. I miss her desperately. It must be terrible for the boys today.

It was difficult to finally turn away from Anna's little body and leave it there in the ICU. Deacons from the church assured me that they would stay with her. Even though her spirit had left the body, now an empty house, it comforted me to know it would not be left alone. Rich, Dan, and Charlie will forever hold my deepest gratitude.

Keith drove us to Grandmother's house in his van, and Pete and Ronn drove Dwight's car. It was a long, silent drive.

When we got here to Grandmother's house, I came upstairs, closed the door, and fell across the bed, finally able to sob, convulsed with weeping. The Psalmist said God keeps our tears in a bottle. He collected a bucket in those moments. Alone before Him, I poured out the overwhelming grief of my heart.

In a little while, a gentle hand rested on my shoulder–Jonathan. We wept together. Soon Dwight joined us, then Josh. We huddled together, clinging to the Love that would not let us go, even in the inky blackness of that hour.

Josh asked, "Are we still triplets?"

Yes, Anna was still his sister and they would always be her brothers. "A cord of three strands is not easily broken." The cord is not broken now, but it is stretched all the way to Heaven, and that hurts.

One by one, each of us will follow Anna to Heaven until all five of us will be there together at last with Jesus, and then we'll never have to do this again.

The only thing that keeps me going now is the promise that Anna waits for us in Heaven and we will see her again.

Dwight said the funeral home appointment was for ten o'clock Monday morning, followed by the cemetery visit. They would need clothes, jewelry, under garments, and a photograph of Anna.

We decided on an outfit I had made for her from scraps of the boys' jeans and bits of crocheted lace for the vest, a cream oxford shirt, and matching soft, dark denim skirt.

I washed and ironed the shirt, ironing the sleeves over and over, knowing it was the last time to iron her clothes. Other things were gathered, including the gold bracelet the boys had given her for their birthday and the emerald ring Josh had bought for her in Texas.

Her last school picture stood between Josh and Jonathan's on top of Grandmother's television downstairs. When Jonathan went down Monday morning, he was alarmed that the picture was missing, concerned we might be removing Anna's pictures now that she was gone. Of course we assured him otherwise.

What about pallbearers? Rob Hanson and Jim Fleshman, for sure. Who of Anna's close friends might be coming from Texas? Mel Young and Jim Davis would be here. Debi said they were, too, so Dr. Tom. Chuck Pace and Kevin Yandell had come to visit at Children's; yes, they were returning for the funeral. One more; Dwight suggested Dennis Toole, a funny Texas yahoo from Southside. Jonathan said later they were exactly who Anna would have chosen.

Miss Dale came to the house Sunday afternoon to receive telephone calls and help with details along with other ladies from the church on following days.

Jonathan accompanied Dwight and me to the funeral home and cemetery to make all arrangements. The funeral director, Ed, and cemetery director, Dave, both knew Anna from television news stories and could not have been more kind. We later learned that Channel 5 news had begun their newscast with a brief announcement that Anna had died.

The casket was cherry wood with carved turnings on all four corners and a cream colored velvet lining. We ordered a casket blanket of peach roses with baby's breath, extra special because since the transplant Anna could not have fresh flowers, which she had always loved.

Bellerive Cemetery is near the church, off the busy Olive Blvd., in a quiet area with winding trails and trees. It is lovely. Mr. Brasfield is buried there, too, and I commented that it must have given him such joy to welcome Anna to Heaven and start showing her around and telling her stories about everybody. Only then did Dwight tell me that Anna had died on Mr. Brasfield's birthday.

We took Josh and Jonathan shopping for new dress clothes, navy sport coats and pleated trousers. They have grown in the past year in every way—physically, emotionally, and spiritually.

The funeral home allowed us to display pictures of Anna, since people here never knew her before she was sick. Jonathan and I got up very early, about 4:30 AM and started poring over the albums, beginning with their infancy in Palestine. So glad the albums were rescued from the fire. After hours of deliberation and memories, we settled on photos of her at various stages and points of interest, many with her brothers.

We could easily have included a hundred more.

My parents and the aunts arrived, and others from out of town, too. One of the most tender parts of the day was a telephone call from Uncle Nub, saying there was someone who wanted to talk to me. He held the phone for Sweet Granny, and she talked like she had ten years earlier. Her voice was strong and clear. She asked if "the girls" had gotten there, wanted to know what I had put on Anna (which clothes), and reminded me that God's grace was sufficient for our need. She also said there was no grief like the loss of a child. Her call was a gift beyond measure.

Family viewing time at the funeral home preceded the public hours. Anna's clothes looked pretty—both boys pointed out strips of their denims between rows of lace trim—but her face was the dearest. After such great suffering, she still wore the sweetest expression. Even her "angel kisses" (freckles) showed through lightly applied powder. Her shiny curls were still soft to the touch.

Josh and Jonathan took particular interest in selecting which flowers should stand closest to the casket—one from their school in Texas, Spring flowers from the Brasfields, and a huge maroon and white spray from Susan and Jim with white ribbons lettered in gold, "Texas A&M."

We were advised to greet visitors quickly as the line was very long. Even so, it continued for over five hours. One employee said he had worked at the funeral home since 1937 and had never seen so many people for a visitation.

Anna was a virtual stranger in St. Louis; her brief time here had been spent almost entirely in the hospital. She was not a Cardinal baseball player or a politician or a social celebrity. "Blessed are the meek . . ."

Many hospital employees, nurses, and physicians came, individually and in small groups, standing for hours in line. Some brought their families, too. We were deeply touched.

Our greatest awe was seeing fellow patients and their families again. Anna's friend Mrs. Tierney came through the line with all her adult children and their families; baby Josh's mommy and daddy; Carolyn Hix; even Kara and her parents and grandparents though she was still in chemotherapy and very sick. They and many others said they had heard about Anna's death and funeral visitation on the television tribute. Their presence meant the world to our family.

Our Parkway family stood by their Pastor and family, faithful and kind as ever. Some identified themselves by the times they had daily prayed—"I was 2:30." Others shared that they had donated blood for Anna. How we love these folks and thank the Lord for bringing us to them.

We dreaded the funeral Wednesday, knowing that would be the final ceremony in the parting process. It was the hottest day of summer—around ninety-five degrees and very humid.

The service was at Parkway by Dwight's request because Anna loved it, and he was right. When we arrived at eleven o'clock, two hours early, we were greeted in the foyer by hugs from old friends from Paris and Palestine. We were unprepared for the great number of them who came, especially since simultaneous services were held in both Palestine and Paris.

After greeting them all, we walked with Bro. Lowrie, our dear pastor, into the sanctuary, where Anna's body already lay in state. Bro. Lowrie married us in 1978 and has been our pastor and Dwight's mentor all these years. Dr. Jim Bryant and Ruby met us at the altar area, too. They are precious. He is a gifted administrator and kept everything on an even keel throughout the funeral.

Many people came to pay respects who had not come to the funeral home, so once again we stood by the casket for two hours receiving condolences.

Joshua and Jonathan stood beside us receiving every guest both at the funeral home and at the church. They greeted everyone with courtesy and respect. It must have been so long and hard for them. What champion brothers and sons they are.

At ten minutes to one, Bro. Lowrie and Dr. Jim stepped up and said, "It's time to go," indicating we were to leave the sanctuary with them. I hesitated, realizing this was the last time to see Anna here on earth—that if I turned away, the casket would be closed, covering her sweet face from view and touch until some faraway time of the resurrection.

"No, not yet," I mumbled. "I'm not ready right now."

"Yes," Bro. Lowrie gently insisted. "It's time."

Turning back to the sleeping cherub face of my beloved child, I tried desperately to memorize every detail—touching her sleeve, stroking her hair, bending to tenderly kiss her soft strands one last time. A final parting touch and we were whisked away through a side door to the choir room.

They brought in the rest of the family delegation. Dr. Jim gave us instructions, Bro. Lowrie prayed, and we filed back into the sanctuary. The four of us sat together on the front pew facing the now-closed coffin.

Anna's service was lovely, a time of real worship to the Creator and thanksgiving for the life of our beloved Anna Joy. Bro. Lowrie spoke powerfully, "The just shall live by faith," the congregation sang "How Firm a Foundation" and "It is Well with My Soul," Dr. Jim read Psalm 23, and Cheri sang "The Lord's Prayer."

Several people shared memories briefly at standing mikes. Cecil Morgan told how he wanted to give the children a registered German shepherd puppy and I wouldn't let him, but the Lord sent them a little orphaned mutt right to our yard instead—"Sweetie." Susan told about the November trip to Texas A&M. Dr. Mike Skinner recounted the time he came into Anna's hospital room and found her unusually listless. He spoke with me instead, then as he turned to go he said, "Hook 'em, horns," and Anna immediately opened her eyes.

After Cheri sang, we followed the casket out and were escorted into the funeral limousine. From the car we were again amazed to see the crowd of people surging out of the church into the parking lot, many we had not seen before. One solitary figure emerged alone, and we gasped to see him—Dr. Dipersio. He caught our eye and came over to the car—a hug for me and a firm, grateful handshake from Dwight. Few words were exchanged, but as he walked away, our hearts were comforted with the hope that God would allow Anna to peek over the banisters of Heaven and know that Dr. Dipersio did come to church after all.

The cemetery service was brief because of the extreme heat. Bro. Lowrie read verses about the assurance of eternal life, then Dr. Jim prayed and led us in singing "Amazing Grace."

Too quickly, it seemed, it was over and we were being ushered out of the tent back toward the car. At the edge of the tent, I paused for one last touch, the corner of the wooden container holding the lifeless body of my darling Anna girl, the final goodbye.

I must have raced from there to the funeral car–vaguely remember Dwight saying "Wait and let me help you." Inside, the cool leather cushions and closed doors were a numbing cocoon from the painful reality of the tent.

Our Parkway family served a sit-down luncheon at the church. That was kind of a blur but very appropriate and so nice. We got to see people like the McKims from North Carolina and Tyres from Cincinnati and others who had come in that morning. There was such an abundance of food and flowers, we sent to shut-ins and families who had other needs.

Returning later to the cemetery by ourselves, we saw how pretty the flowers were piled on top of the fresh grave. We took the Aggie ribbons back for Anna's scrapbook, and Josh asked if we could take some flowers to Mr. Brasfield's grave.

It's now three o'clock. I've been writing all day except for a few breaks for telephone calls and tissues. The boys will be home from school soon. Need to shower and dress and cook them a good dinner.

The Lord is good.

GRAPPLING

THURSDAY, AUGUST 29

Several people told us that time would help, that we should allow our grief sufficient time. Last night I slept soundly for the first time, probably close to six hours. Such a blessing.

I went through a plastic storage basket of Anna's yesterday containing bits and pieces of her personal things, and found a beautiful poem, written in her own hand, entitled "Good-bye." It is almost like a little note from her to me, although I'm sure it was her heart's expression at leaving her friends in Texas. Must have been an English assignment; there's a red "100" marked in the corner.

There was also a box of school notes from her friends, each one folded in unique, creative ways. I was briefly tempted to open and read them but decided they had been private before and should remain so, so I threw them all away.

Her purse and little odds and ends are such dear links to her, even the opened package of Sweet Tarts she picked up next to the cash register on our happy expedition to "Wally World." I keep it here next to my chair tucked out of sight from anyone else—just reach and touch them every once in a while.

Each of the Aunts has called and are so comforting. Aunt Rachel said she didn't dream about Uncle Robert for two or three years after his death. I miss Anna most at bedtime. That was always a special time for prayers and hugs and meaningful talks. Even when she did spend the night away from home, she always called back to say "good-night." I have hoped that maybe one of these nights I might see her sweet smiling face in a dream saying "Good night, Mom."

SATURDAY, AUGUST 31

Yesterday was the hardest day yet. I washed a few more of her things in the basket with our other family laundry, and in it was her soft, worn volleyball shirt. I hugged it to my cheek and wept for her again. All day I thought of her, healthy and strong, always smiling and laughing, with her gorgeous mane of red hair. It's a blessing to remember her that way rather than the sick little invalid I cared for during the past year.

All day as I gathered our things for this week-end getaway, there was a lingering sense that for the first time we were packing for four instead of five.

SUNDAY, SEPTEMBER 1

It's been a wonderful week-end in many ways, especially being off with Dwight and the boys. I miss Anna terribly, but the Lord gives grace to somehow get through the hardest times. Tears are always just barely below the surface. I try to control them most of the time.

Everything reminds me of Anna. It must get better at some point. Everyone says it does. Lord, help me, please.

WEDNESDAY, SEPTEMBER 4

The van is loaded down with Anna's things to be taken away–shopping bags of clothes and shoes in the back for Salvation Army, medical supplies in front for the special summer camp for children with cancer, packages to mail for a few of her special friends in Texas.

Even though I kept some of Anna's most favorite clothes and other things, it is difficult to part with anything she touched or wore. As I came back in the front door a few minutes ago, my eye was drawn to the purple and green banner high up on the wall of Anna's little room above the windows, "I can do all things through Christ who strengthens me." It was on her hospital walls last year and we put it up here when she came home after the transplant before the seizures. It's His Word to me today. Depend on Him. Lean on Him. Rest in Him.

I'm ready to begin the mammoth thank-you notes venture.

THURSDAY, SEPTEMBER 19

"But as for me, I trust in the Thee, O Lord. I say, 'Thou art My God.' My times are in Thy hand." Psalm 31:14–15.

Our Psalm 31 reading this morning at breakfast included the familiar passage we had posted on the wall of Anna's room last summer–light blue paper cut about two inches wide in a circle taped around the big round clock in her room.

How many times did I look at that verse and repeat it back to the Lord. We left it and some others in the bone marrow unit after the transplant for other patients.

Now I read it again from the other side. Anna is gone. My grief knows no bounds. How much anguish can the human heart endure? I function normally (it seems) with meals, laundry, shopping, etc. Attend every service at the church, meeting and speaking to all the people. Often hear how "strong" I am, and try to smile while I am dying inside. Have written almost three hundred notes of thanks and am not nearly finished. Help the boys with schoolwork, four papers to proof today.

But it is always there—the deep, dark, aching pain, the gaping wound left bleeding where the cherished little girl of my heart has been ripped away. If only I could hold her close one more time, tell her that I love her, see her sweet smile. Never again on this earth.

O, Lord, I do trust You, but the pain is so great that it sometimes overwhelms conscious thought and reasoning. I am drowning in this sea of sorrow.

Was Anna's life here cut short as punishment for my sin? Has the wickedness of the mother been avenged in the death of the child? Did the insect spray in her bedroom cause leukemia? The microwave oven? Sitting too close to the television for "Sesame Street"? Did I pray too little? Not read enough Scripture? Have too little faith?

In her last weeks, when her physical condition was perilous and sedation for her breathing became increasingly fragile, did she know that I was sitting beside her, keeping the promise that she would never be alone? Did she hurt? Was she afraid?

Last year in November just after returning to the hospital at the first seizure, the night before the second terrible seizure that left her in a coma, Anna prayed aloud from her hospital bed, "Lord, thank You for Your peace that passes understanding."

That comes to mind now. Must be the Lord's Spirit whispering comfort to my troubled heart. Perhaps Anna herself is asking the Lord to please help her poor Mama, although surely He would not let her see my tears.

"But as for me, I trust in Thee, O Lord. I say, 'Thou art my God.' My times are in Thy hand." As we read it this morning, we compared it to our own parent/child relationships.

I asked Josh and Jonathan if there had ever been times when they asked for something to be done a certain way and Mother denied it. What was their reaction? Did they happily skip away, laughing and singing? Did they fall down on the floor in anger and have a head-banging tantrum? Or did they learn quiet submission, showing respect to the role of the parent, who ultimately wanted only the best for the individual child and for the family?

Granted, Mom had and has only the most finite wisdom. The Lord, our Father, has all wisdom.

They learned to endure disappointment. They learned to wait for some future good they could not see at the time.

Questions? Yes.

Frustration? Sometimes.

Resolution? Always. Even though Mother said "No."

Dwight and I and multitudes of others pleaded with God to let Anna live. He granted her, and us, one extra year; then He took her. We were still begging Him to let her stay, but He gently yet firmly answered "No."

Now I am the child and He is the Heavenly Parent. I have implored Him with my whole heart, yet He has said "No," with the finality of a coffin and the "someday" promise of the resurrection.

Lord, give me grace to trust You with a sweeter will than ever before. Teach me that Anna's times were in Your sovereign hands, as are mine and those of Joshua, Jonathan, and Dwight. Thou art my God. Subdue my petulance. Heal my brokenness. Restore to me the joy of Thy salvation. Bless us as a family to know and share Your love, the love of a Father Who gave His only Son.

Shugie called a few minutes ago from Florida. She's scheduled to lead a seminar on prayer this week-end and is grappling with Anna's death in light of the many prayers of believers everywhere for her and the great multitude of unbelievers looking on.

I thanked her for the prayers and shared from yesterday's journal entry.

God is faithful. Period. Nothing that enters the lives of His children is apart from His faithfulness, including the illness and death of a little girl. Yes, I grieve, but not as those who have no hope. The "blessed hope" is the assurance that someday we will join Anna in Heaven with Jesus for eternity.

Last summer and again in the winter He heard the prayers. "You know, so many of My children are begging, and the Mama could really use a little more time. Let's give her another year." And He did. We asked Him to heal her cancer. It was gone.

But on August 18, Anna's days were up, and even though people prayed, He said "No." Not a brutal, uncaring "no," but a gentle denial accompanied by divine grace commensurate for the immense need. Now He patiently cares for my wounded heart and continues to carry us forward toward the completed picture we cannot see from this side.

TUESDAY, SEPTEMBER 24, 1996–BIRTHDAY

"The Lord is near to the brokenhearted and saves those who are crushed in spirit." Psalm 34:18.

Today is the children's birthday, born in 1981, fifteen years ago, tiny preemies at Baylor Hospital in Dallas. How we have thanked God through all these fifteen years for His deliverance then and His miraculous blessing to give them full, healthy lives. Little did we ever imagine Anna would on this birthday be in Heaven.

Lord, give us grace for this day. Hold us up with Your strong arms. Let Your unwavering mercy sustain us as we rejoice in the youthful vigor of our fine sons and remember the loveliness of our daughter who is now with You. Give us truly thankful hearts for the magnificent gifts You entrusted to our care in those three treasures.

According to tradition begun in kindergarten, Josh and Jonathan placed orders for lunch, this year Subway and Burger King, to be delivered at the school cafeteria by both Dad and me. In the past we have eaten birthday lunch together, but perhaps not this year as teenagers. They've asked for Papa John's veggie pizza tonight. Have tickets to see Ozzie Smith play his final game Saturday for the Cardinals.

Last Thursday night Dwight and I went to a parents' meeting at Westminster to meet the teachers. In the math classroom, Mr. Vonder Bruegge pointed to a large sign on the wall as he enlightened us parents, "There's only one rule in my classroom, and that's it (pointing): NO SNIVELING."

Good rule. Lord, grant me grace to grieve without sniveling.

FRIDAY, OCTOBER 4

The Aunts tell me Sweet Granny is dying, in the hospital semi-conscious and the doctor says now slipping into a coma. Josh and Jonathan's school is out today, so we had already planned to drive down to see her. The Aunts felt it would be better for me to wait and come with Dwight. They said to bring Sunday/funeral clothes.

She has given me an example of godliness, living the walk of faith and showing us the love of Jesus. Anna and Granny were special buddies, "kindred spirits." Their birthdays were only three days apart, September 24 and 27. This year Uncle

Earl planted two Bradford pear trees side by side for them at the Evergreen church cemetery. Wish I could snuggle into her soft lap again as so many times in childhood. I love you, Granny.

Thank you for showing Jesus to me.

SATURDAY, OCTOBER 5

We were with Sweet Granny as she joined Anna in Heaven. Now they are together for eternity. What a pair. My heart aches at her loss, but it is not as searing as the loss of Anna. In fact, there is a strange sort of comfort in knowing that they are together for eternity. She was precious. Earth's loss really is Heaven's gain.

MONDAY, NOVEMBER 25

Amy's wedding rehearsal was a greater challenge than I had expected, especially seeing her bridesmaids coming down the aisle. She remembered Anna beautifully in the printed order of service and asked me to pray with her and Kris at the altar during the service. For the dinner I was seated with Sharon and Bill, next to Mary Lynn and her daughters. Embarrassed myself with tears, but they just would not stop.

The wedding was an experience of worship as Amy and Kris dedicated their marriage to the Lord. She looked like Cinderella. Anna would have loved it. I had to keep reminding myself that Heaven is better. Nothing here compares.

Kristen decorated a gazebo in the church gym with curtain sheers and white lights, so beautiful. She is a jewel. Sharon had collected red rose petals in big baskets for little girls to carry after the wedding. Guests reached for a handful and threw those for the get-away. I kept hoping the Lord let Anna look over us and see it all. Isn't that "the great cloud of witnesses" from Hebrews? I think so.

Back at Aunt Dorisy's house in the comfort and quiet of her dear nest. Thank You, Father.

I've been reflecting on a quote from Mary Lynn scribbled on a napkin at the rehearsal dinner. "God's children do not live by explanation; they live by God's promise."

It's true.

"GOODBYE"
BY ANNA JOY BLANKENSHIP

Goodbye, a word so hard to say.

Goodbye, should be so far away.

Goodbye, comes closer every day.

Who lives to say goodbye?

We love

We learn

We live our days

And still the parting comes.

The word deems not to cross man's lips

But tears his heart instead.

We whisper the word,

"Don't go" is said.

Goodbye brings tears

Goodbye brings hurt

Its sorrow does not cease.

But bound with time

The wound will heal

And man's soul will find peace.

"Goodbye" and "Memories" were written as seventh grade English assignments as Anna faced the prospect of moving from Texas to St. Louis.

"WHY DO PEOPLE DIE?"

BY ANNA JOY BLANKENSHIP

Why do people die?
They live, they laugh,
they walk and talk,
and suddenly
how still they lie.

Their face, how pale
it was before
from fighting the dreadful sickness,
now looks happy.

Victory! It seems to say.
Oh, what a glorious day.

Your heart seems to be
in your throat.
Your eyes fill with tears.
They've lost all their fears.
You know they're not suffering now.

They are with their Heavenly Father
Who loves them by and by.

Only He has the perfect plan.

That's why people die.

This poem was written by Anna, entirely on her own, in the summer of 1993 when she was eleven years old. She was happy and healthy. The original hand-scrawled manuscript was in red marker on bright blue paper.

EPILOGUE

The months and years following Anna's death brought gradual healing to our broken hearts although Anna's tender spot will always remain.

People who say time is a great healer have probably been there. The pain of missing Anna has never gone away, but it has become bearable. We remember her place in our family with deepest love and gratitude, and have found ways to honor her memory as part of our own journey. This book is one example.

One of my greatest concerns was how Joshua and Jonathan might be affected by the traumatic disruption of their young lives. They had come to St. Louis moving to a new city, new school, new church, without their sister (who was the hub of the wheel), and without their mother in the home. Dad was stretched to care for them, look after Grandmother's needs, pastor the church, and see us at the hospital.

Two weeks after Anna died, Labor Day weekend, I tried to express to the boys regret for what must have been a very difficult time for them. I wanted them to know that we loved each child equally, and that if sickness had come to one of them instead of to Anna, we would have responded as a family in the same way. I was so very sorry to have left them alone.

Jonathan's response touched my heart to the core and showed maturity well beyond his years. I recorded it that night in the journal word for word.

"Mom," he said, "You've told us before lots of times that you loved us all the same, but I never realized how much you loved me until I saw you with Anna. When I saw how much you loved her, I realized how much you must love me, too."

Romans 8:28, "And we know that God causes all things to work together for good to those who love Him, to those who are called according to His purpose."

God promises that if we truly love Him, He will cause even the most terrible things in our lives to somehow be used for good. This has been true for us. Take the house, for instance.

During Anna's illness she and I collected pictures snipped from each month's *Better Homes and Gardens* magazine, ideas we might use for the house in Missouri the Lord would surely provide someday. Our possessions salvaged from the fire were scattered to the four winds among good church members. Things damaged beyond repair had been discarded. We didn't have a clue what was where and decided to "count all things as loss for the sake of Christ Jesus" and be grateful for whatever turned up.

The last issue Anna and I perused was August, 1996, available in July. Pictured on its cover was a great screened porch which we agreed would be perfect for cooler Missouri summer evenings. When Anna died August 18 and personal effects in our

ICU cubicle collected, that magazine was among things taken back to Grandmother's house with us on that saddest of days.

Spring, 1997, after Anna's death the previous August, our house in Texas was finally rebuilt from the fire and sold, so Dwight and I began looking for a new place in St. Louis. When our friend and realtor Judy Hale took me to look at houses, my invariable response was, "Yes, this will work," to which she would say, "No, this is not the one for you." Quite a role reversal in real estate.

One morning Judy drove me along for the realtor's tour of new listings and, as before, I liked everything we saw. At the third house she paused the car at the driveway and said, "I think this may be the one."

Judy and I both loved the house, and she said we must offer a contract that day, because it was sure to sell. Dwight was in a downtown meeting with no beepers and I would never buy a house without him. Undaunted, Judy instructed me to try to reach him while she busily typed a contract. To our amazement, Dwight had left his meeting early, was at the church, and would come right over to join us.

While Dwight and Judy inspected the house, I sat on the beautiful shaded back screened porch with the selling realtor. It seemed perfect. "If my husband likes it, we're going to buy this house," I told her.

"Do you ever read *Better Homes and Gardens?*" she asked, motioning to a copy of the magazine on a white wicker table before us.

It was the August, 1996 issue, the last one Anna and I had saved. The familiar picture on the front cover resembled the porch where we sat.

"I have this magazine. The porch here looks like this one. Did they copy it for this porch?"

She gave a knowing smile. "This is the porch."

It was. This was the porch Anna and I had admired and saved in our last happy days together. Coincidence? I'll never think so. The gracious owners received three contracts that day and accepted ours. In ways that we did not understand, God was "working things together" for our good.

By the way, some experts advise people in grief not to take major steps for at least one year. In our case, the owners selling the house placed one stipulation on the sale. Because they were facing an out-of-state transfer, they required a delayed closing date for the sale, which they had already set, August 18, exactly one year after Anna's death.

Joshua and Jonathan were thrilled after almost three years since the fire to be in our own home. On the first evening they bounded through the house in boxer shorts jumping and laughing, "We're home!"

They finished high school at Westminster Christian Academy, and as graduation approached I wondered if they thought of their sister. After the ceremony friends gathered for picture taking and congratulations, but Jonathan was missing. When we opened the kitchen door at home a little while later, Jonathan sat at the table calmly eating a bowl of cereal. He looked up at Josh and said to hurry and change clothes so they could leave. There was plenty of time before the graduation party, but Jonathan quietly let me know they had something to do and please not to ask questions.

I noticed that as the boys left they reached for a flashlight.

The next day when I went to the cemetery, carefully laid on the grass of Anna's grave were two long-stemmed yellow roses of Texas.

A cord of three strands is not easily broken.

Jonathan completed a University of Missouri graduate program in bio-statistics and now works in cancer research in Pennsylvania. After the United States Marines, Josh became a Texas A&M Aggie and remains in Texas, working in business logistics.

Dwight still shepherds Parkway Baptist Church as the senior pastor. God has blessed his faithful ministry in this loving congregation, a true "household of faith." He still roots for the Cardinals, too! We earnestly thank God for our Parkway family.

With Dwight's encouragement and Parkway's blessing, I trained, became board certified, and was called to Missouri Baptist Medical Center, serving as lead chaplain.

REFLECTIONS

It has been twelve years since Anna's diagnosis, eleven since her death. During these years of missing her and gradually learning to live again, I have walked with others through their own grief experiences and reflected on my own. Here are a few common threads.

EVERY PERSON'S GRIEF IS UNIQUE.
Grief is the response to loss. Any loss can trigger grief—loss of a marriage, loss of a job, loss of anything. Each loss is unique in any given situation. An individual comes to the grief experience with his/her own personality, life experience, and circumstances. Because of that, each of us will and must grieve in our own way.

During Anna's illness and death, Dwight and I responded in different ways. So did Josh and Jonathan, whose loss as triplet brothers was profound. Each of us loved her dearly, comforted one another in her loss, and found personal ways to express our grief and work toward healing.

One person will cry, another will not. One talks, the other is silent. One will work to a frenzy, the other will sit. One needs company, while the other craves solitude. One goes to the cemetery, another never returns. Others will eat or spend or panic or laugh or combinations of all of the above at various times.

On any given day, the mourner may seem inconsistent to oneself and to others. That's O.K. Your grief is your own. Trust God to carry you through it however you must.

THERE ARE NO SHORTCUTS THROUGH GRIEF.
The grief experience is a process. Soon after Anna died, I said to Dwight, "I know I will survive and somehow carry on, but I will never be happy again." It was a time of such bewilderment, joy and light seemed very far away. Waves of sorrow would roll over my heart, and when a wave receded, the gaping hole of "missing" still ached.

I knew that Anna was in Heaven and that we would see her again, but oh, how I missed her with every fiber of my being.

By God's grace, very gradually, the healing process began and the pain of missing was accompanied by smiles from sweet memories. It took time and tears and work.

Unlike the healing of a skinned knee, the hurt in our broken hearts did not consistently improve every day until the pain was gone. There would be better days and then bummer days. In fact, there were times in the second year I wondered if my grief was any better at all. It took a monumental effort to get back to the business of living with many "time outs" for weeping.

Review of journals from subsequent years reveals that although Anna's loss still hurt, it became less paramount. Other concerns and interests and, yes, joys began to emerge, too.

Someone told me recently if you have a hundred and twenty-five tears to cry, a hundred and twenty-four are not enough. Allow yourself and others the time and tears necessary to journey through grief.

SYMPTOMS OF GRIEF ARE REAL.

The September 19, 1996 journal entry lists some weird possibilities of how I might have caused Anna's leukemia or omissions that might have saved her. I remember asking Dr. Rob Hanson if any of those things could have contributed to her sickness or death. He leaned down from his considerable height advantage, looked me straight in the eye, and emphatically answered, "No." He went on to explain that every parent of a child with cancer asks those questions.

Grief is often accompanied by guilt. Deserved or not, it is real. Widows have shared with me the guilt they feel related to their husbands' deaths. Did I feed him badly? Did I add to his stress? Did he know that I loved him? Why him and not me?

A plethora of "if onlys." One of Dwight's favorite maxims: "If ifs and buts were candy and nuts, we'd all have a merry Christmas."

Often people who are grieving express, "I am so tired." Fatigue is another of the symptoms that commonly come with grief. Others include forgetfulness, confusion, irritability, sleeplessness, and changes in eating patterns.

Already prone to forgetfulness, my inclination seemed even greater after Anna's death. "Great," I thought. "Dwight has lost his child and now his wife is crackers."

It was a relief to realize I was not losing my mind but going through some normal responses to grief. Give yourself and others some slack when you or they seem a little unbalanced after the loss. It is normal.

SYMBOLS AND RITUALS CAN HELP.

At a Jewish gravesite, mourners are invited to take a turn with a shovel of dirt. They may lay a stone of remembrance. They often observe "sitting shiva," when the family remains inside the house for as many as ten days while friends come and go with food and fond recollections of the loved one who has died.

Young parents of a stillborn baby name the child and cherish the toes of his or her inked footprint.

Other parents remember their children by releasing balloons, which forever become associated with the departed spirit of the one they loved.

A snippet of aged white hair tied with ribbon is tucked away.

The special recipe for banana pudding or chicken dumplings is faithfully passed down and created again and again in memory of a beloved grandmother.

A tree may be planted to honor a loved one. A garden. A sculpture. An engraved marker. A namesake. A memorial gift.

Through the years, Anna and I gave each other gifts with hearts on them. It was a symbol of our love for one another. Little dresses I made for her always had a heart in the fabric or lace or a button or embroidered inside the hem. Heart tokens she gave me are lasting reminders. In selecting a cemetery grave marker for her, we included the symbol of a heart. It comforted us because it was a special symbol for Anna.

Rituals and symbols often overlap; a symbol may be part of a ritual and vice versa.

The Cross is a symbol for us of Jesus. When we see a cross as jewelry or architectural design, it reminds us of His sacrificial death and resurrection.

Jesus also used the symbols of bread and the cup to represent His own death. Their use became a ritual of remembrance following His instruction, "Do this in remembrance of Me." We may neglect thoughts of His sacrifice, but that ritual from His last Passover Supper never lets us forget His supreme act of love.

Rituals like the funeral service are for one time. Others become tradition, like Memorial Day. Some rituals are for a season.

Because Anna loved flowers but was unable to enjoy them after her transplant, it was important to me that her grave had fresh flowers. Every Sunday morning before church I would stop at the market for a bouquet, then drive to the cemetery, walk up the hill, and place flowers and water in the holder at her grave. In August heat, they would soon burn and need replacement before the following Sunday. In winter cold they would often freeze the same day. I remember driving through the cemetery to the spot nearest her grave and seeing only one set of footprints through the snow—my own from the day before. The ritual was meaningful but eventually gave way to more suitable silk flowers—and daffodil bulbs, which bloom every Spring.

For Thanksgiving after Anna died in August, Josh asked if we could go to Chicago. It was strange to wander around the immense aquarium there, the only attraction open Thanksgiving Day and the only English-speaking Americans touring it, but we remember the experience fondly. Did we give thanks? Yes. Did it stunt every Thanksgiving afterward? No, it was for a season, and since then we have observed traditional Thanksgivings with turkey and dressing.

Judicious use of symbols and rituals can help bring comfort immediately and in years to come.

WE ARE NOT ALONE.
"Blessed be the God and Father of our Lord Jesus Christ, the Father of mercies and the God of all comfort; Who comforts us in all our affliction so that we may be able to comfort those who are in any affliction with the comfort with which we ourselves are comforted by God." II Corinthians 1:3–4.

Although every grief experience is unique, God often uses other people who have shared similar experiences to offer comfort.

When Anna was dying, senior adults Beatty and Ruthie Miller came to the hospital and remained in the waiting room the night before she passed away. Their young son Curtis had died many years before after a long illness. I was deeply comforted by their presence and care because I knew they understood better than anyone else where we were. It must have cost them emotionally to go with us through the valley, but their kind support meant so much.

During Anna's illness and afterward Aunt Rachel offered comfort from her experience with Uncle Robert's terminal cancer. He was not her child, but it was cancer, and at many levels she had "been there" and understood. One morning after Anna died Aunt Rachel called long distance and I apologized for crying. She said, "It's O.K. Don't hang up. I'll stay on the line with you. Just cry."

And I did. She stayed on the phone while I cried and cried and cried. From hundreds of miles away she held me close. Others also cared, but Aunt Rachel had experienced the pain of loss.

While I had always felt sympathy for people who lost loved ones, my ministry to them is different now. Be willing to embrace comfort from fellow pilgrims. One day you will be able to help someone else.

THIS IS THE TIME TO RECEIVE.
How awkward I felt when young seminarian Peter Beck extended his open hand to take my soggy tissue, but he kindly insisted and later professed that it was his greatest lesson in real ministry.

The Bible says, "Bear ye one another's burdens, and so fulfill the law of Christ." If we do not allow others to help us, we are denying them the opportunity to obey Christ.

At some time the person in grief may need privacy, solitude. Or advice. Or "ministry of presence." Or any of a hundred other things. If your friends are not mind readers, share with them honestly.

Simple needs thoughtfully met can mean a world of difference in time of grief. Someone appears at the door with food. Another, unnoticed, mows the front lawn. Clothes are slipped to the dry cleaners. These are the hands of Christ reaching out to help in your time of distress. Say "thank you" and let them.

THE HURT NEVER GOES COMPLETELY AWAY, BUT IT DOES BECOME BEARABLE.

"When will I stop missing my loved one?"

For most of us, never. But the acute, searing pain of fresh grief does finally abate.

I promise.

There will always be a tender spot in my heart for Anna. Josh and Jonathan are outstanding sons, and we pray that someday the Lord will bless them to marry wonderful young women and even to bring grandchildren. Every day my spirit is watered by special relationships with women of all ages. But there is a place in my heart that is just for Anna, and it always will be. Where once her memory brought anguish, now there is a sweet fragrance of her, a sigh of missing, and the promise of seeing her again.

New days bring new life chapters. Acceptance and gratitude are part of healing. The tender spot remains because you will always remember your loved one. As healing comes, let cherished memories nurture your spirit and remind you that God's mercy is fresh every morning.

EVERYTHING HERE IS TEMPORARY. HEAVEN IS ETERNAL.
That sounds melancholy, even religiously trite, but is so very true. The Bible says life is a vapor, a flower that blooms and then as quickly is gone. Both my grandmothers lived to be almost one hundred years old. Almost a century. Long life? What is a hundred years in the span of eternity?

Several years ago Dwight was invited to speak in England for a pastor's conference, and while we were there I visited children in a local elementary school to talk about American culture. One picture was of the Alamo, the bedrock of Texas history. Very politely, a little boy raised his hand to clarify that their school building in which we sat was older than the Alamo! Our view of time is skewed by human finitude.

The stuff of life here seems like ultimate reality because it is all we see and know. But when at death we pass over to the other side, we will finally understand that "real" life is there in Heaven. "Eye has not seen nor ear heard, neither has entered the heart of man, all that God has prepared for those who love Him" II Corinthians 2:9.

The Bible says now we "see through a glass darkly." We know that Heaven exists, but it is still a mystery to us, like looking through a cloudy window. "Faith is the evidence of things not seen." We believe it though we have not seen it.

How many years have you lived on this earth? How quickly are the eras of your life speeding by? Anna and others who have already passed from earth to Heaven know that their experience on earth was only a blink of an eye compared with real life in their eternal home. One day soon we will join them there in the presence of Christ where forever there will be no more "good-byes."

Looking at life with an eternal perspective gives us hope and confidence for the day when we meet Jesus face to face and see our loved ones again.

I CAN TRUST THE FAITHFULNESS OF GOD.

"Why?" Anna's friends and nurses and doctors and mother asked during and after her long struggle and death. Why cancer? Why someone so good and kind and intelligent and young as Anna? Why???

I don't know. I honestly don't know.

But I have thought about it and even wrestled with it until it was just too much for this soul and mind.

And I have decided to trust God. I believe He is faithful and just, that He loved and still loves Anna, and that He loves Dwight and Josh and Jonathan and me. I will never understand the "why's" of pain and suffering, "why" sin was allowed to enter the earth, "why" Jesus, God's own Son, suffered and died on the Cross for our sin, but I choose to trust Him.

During Anna's last night on earth, I sat next to her bed and thought and prayed and remembered. As the respirator whooshed artificial breaths into her frail body, I stroked her wispy strands of hair and remembered that shining mass of red waves, her bright happy eyes and ready smile. How had we come to this moment? How could I ever face life without her?

In those hours, I silently considered what God had done for us in the death of His own Son, Jesus.

God had given me, a "barren" woman, three beautiful children.

He had only one.

Anna was offered pain medication at every turn. Even when she refused it, I implored, "Please don't let her hurt."

God's Son endured the most horrible death by crucifixion ever known in human experience before or since.

With my reminders, Anna's modesty was strictly observed. Even in a coma, she was always shown respect.

Jesus, God's Son, was shamefully stripped and then nailed to the cross, raised high on a hill as a public spectacle for all the world to see.

Anna and our family were supported throughout her ordeal by the kindness and prayers of many people, some of whom we never met.

When Jesus hung on the cross, most of the disciples hid or ran away.

As we drove through the night from Texas after Anna's diagnosis, I promised never to leave her. She would not be alone. By God's grace it was a promise kept.

The most poignant passage in the Bible for me is the cry of Jesus from the cross, "Abba, Father, Daddy, why have you forsaken me?"

God the Father had to turn away from his only beloved Son as he suffered and then died. Agony for the Father and the Son must have been facing that dreadful hour apart from one another.

I did not want to give Anna up. We tried everything—chemotherapy, radiation, the transplant, natural juices, someone even called about giving her ground shark fins. Dwight fasted and prayed for forty days. If we could have prevented her death in any way, we would have.

If I could have given Anna's life in exchange for yours, dear reader, I would not have done it, even as exchange for the life of your child or anyone else's.

And I for sure would never have offered Anna's sweet life for the life of some hoodlum out on the street.

But God did.

God looked down and saw Sherry Ann—selfish, sinful, insignificant, with nothing good to claim.

"She's doomed; she'll never make it by herself." And so He allowed His only Son, Jesus, to die. Not just any death, but death on the Cross, nails in His hands and feet, the just for the unjust, to bring us to God. That, my friend, is love.

After Anna died, sometimes well-meaning people would ask, "Aren't you really, *really* angry with God?" That is often the case as a person grapples with the excruciating pain of loss, and God certainly understands and cares.

I did ask "why" and sometimes wallowed in self-pity, but deep down I could never quite feel rage toward a God who loved me and loved Anna so much. He never required as much of me as He did of Himself in the death of His own Son. Why would I want to be even temporarily estranged from the loving Father whose care was my peace and solace? Instead of raising my fist to Him, I wanted to be lifted up into His great soft lap and feel His everlasting arms around me holding me close. I found myself crying, "Oh, Father, please help me. Please hold me. It hurts, Lord. Please help me."

I can tell you now, dear reader, there is no other real peace for the troubled soul than the peace He offers.

When the children were small, we used to tape colorful pictures and posters on the refrigerator at their eye level. One morning it was a page clipped from their Sunday School leaflet, a colored sketch of Jesus blessing the little children.

Here came the trio trailing up to the fridge to check it out, Anna in the lead. She stuck a pudgy finger out toward the picture, her red curls bobbing, and said clearly, "Jesus."

Standing nearby, my heart was thrilled to hear His name from her cherub lips.

Alongside her came triplet Jonathan, his bright eyes shining as he, too, pointed with recognition, "Jesus!" A big smile on his precious face reflected the wonder of that sweet moment.

Next Joshua came lumbering up to the fridge in his unique toddler style. He paused, looked, then pointed with a happy grin to the little boy in Jesus's lap. "Joshie!"

It took a second for his message to sink in; but when it did, I dropped to my knees at the realization. He was right. He was exactly, profoundly right.

The child in Jesus's lap was Joshie. And it was Sherry Ann. And it is you.

That little Sunday School paper, after rotating off the fridge, was tucked into my Bible where it has remained for more than twenty years. It's yellowed now, especially the dried-up Scotch tape still folded back, but every time I gently retrieve it from the cover of my rebound Bible it reminds me again of the lesson Jesus taught us so long ago.

How many times through the years have I returned to that tender lesson to claim the warmth and security of our Lord's waiting lap, the gentle embrace of His everlasting arms, a sure shelter from life's storms.

Today His loving arms are extended to you. He invites you, dear child, to crawl up into His lap and to know, once and for all, His grace, His forgiveness, His "peace that passes understanding."

God bless you as you seek and find Him.